ZERO TO AUTHENTIC HERO

The 7 Key Steps to Become a True Leader

Nick Bradley

Zero To Authentic Hero
The 7 Key Steps To Become A <u>True</u> Leader

ISBN-13: 978-1722918682
ISBN-10: 1722918683

The information given in this book should not be treated as a substitute for professional medical advice; always consult a medical practitioner. Any use or information in this book is that the readers discretion and risk. Neither the author nor the publisher can be held responsible for any loss, claim or damage arising out of the use, or misuse, of the suggestions made, the failure to take medical advice or for any material on third party websites.

Published by:
Waldegrave House Ltd
116 Pall Mall
London
SW1Y 5ED
UK

Contents

Alexander & Benjamin
With love from Daddy x

Testimonials

"I now speak with an authentic inner strength. I found my direction, I have clarity of my value. I was playing small, and that was bringing me pain. I am now committed to playing big! Wherever someone is on their leadership journey, this will have a profound effect on them."
Jane Cuthbert, HR Director.

"I'm head and shoulders ahead of where I would have been without this process, and so glad we have acknowledgement of the past and have created a purpose to work together."
Dr. Tom Milligan, Partner, Practice One.

"After 100 days, I have a clearer idea of what needs to be done and what should be said, and how. I have more time to help and encourage my colleagues."
Shanthy Lal, Finance Director. Thornton's Budgens.

"I focus better on priorities now, rather than simply trying to get through emails and calls.
I've found a way to step back and think things through more effectively."
Jan Peacock, Practice Manager, NHS.

"Nick Bradley has become a mindful leader, perfectly blending an executive background with compassion, listening, and gentleness as he inspires and supports others in identifying the best course of action to grow out of any challenge."
Michael Scattergood, Senior Manager EY.

"You let me discover things for myself in small steps that had eluded me before, so that I could piece them together and make substantial changes, and move to a level of performance."
Nigel Long, Professional Services.

"It was an eye-opener. The coaching exceeded expectations because it asked me to take responsibility for changing the way I worked. I focused on finding out about me and how I'd got there. Everything came from within, not from external pressure."
Andrew Voase, Assistant Manager, NHS

Foreword

I am extremely impressed by Nick Bradley's business and leadership experience, which includes over 30 years in financial services and management consulting in the city of London. Nick has leveraged this experience, along with a leading global business school qualification and significant personal development work, that has resulted in a 7 key step process to becoming a true leader.

This whole encompassing and rounded process will challenge and support you to transform your leadership life, giving you clarity of purpose, solid values and a far better understanding of your own skills and resources. This will lead to lower stress, better relationships, and the ability to achieve much more in your leadership life.

Nick's personal story of transformation over the last few years has already inspired many leaders to become truly authentic. His impact continues to ripple throughout the world and his message will inspire you to become a better leader.

This book is a must read if you have taken on a leadership role, or indeed are aspiring to do so, in any business, organization or community, as it will lead you to a place of deep reflection and understanding of self. You will create a powerful 100-day action plan and provide ongoing support so that you can implement the changes in your leadership life.

Raymond Aaron
New York Times Bestselling Author

Free Bonuses

I have made many free bonuses available to you
simply by going to the website:

ZeroToAuthenticHero.com

Free videos covering each of the Steps 1–7.

Worksheets for Steps 1–7
Full size, full colour, ready to print worksheets
which you will need for each step
for you to complete online or fill in by hand.

The 100 Day Plan
Full size, full colour, ready to print worksheet
for you to complete online or fill in by hand.

In addition, you will find access to the
Mandala Leaders Circle
of other leaders who have been through this program
and made a commitment to support you.

ZeroToAuthenticHero.com

Acknowledgements

In this section of my book, I am delighted to share thanks to many of those people who have helped me on my journey, through good times and tough, and out again on the other side. Thank you also to those who have helped in the development of this book and the Mandala Leaders business and sports leadership coaching business. I haven't had space to mention everyone, but you know who you are!!!

Starting with my one of my oldest school friends, **Ian Young**, with whom I have the fondest memories of playing childhood rugby together and talking through school lessons together as we studied to retake our French 'O' Levels, after failing the first time, because of spending too much time talking in class.

Through my time in the work environment, I wanted to thank **Steve Barningham** who always showed the most genuine care and concern for my wellbeing whilst I was running meetings lasting through several days and nights, to deliver complex restructuring deals. **Steve Cockell** and **Andy Turbutt** in the corporate side of the organisation not only gave me good jobs but gave me the space and time to become successful in them.

I will always be grateful to the whole team at **Penninghame House**, led by **Ray & Marie Butler** and **Gordon & Maria Jessiman,** all of whom have invested significant time in supporting me and helping me to learn enough about myself to be able to write a book about it!! They have been beautifully supported by such a wide number of people, all of whom have touched my heart at some time during our work together, including **Venu Sanz** with whom I shared a wonderful week in the kitchen.

The men of the **ManKind Project** have brought me from tears of anger and sadness to tears of joy in one of the most unusual and freeing 15 minutes of my life, and special thanks to all of the men in Richmond and Yorkshire for their continued support.

My short time at the **One World Academy** has to be shared as an immensely freeing and deeply connecting experience, and I have to thank **Krishnaji & Preethaji** for all of their amazing work, and **Gaynor & Mal King** for their huge love, and very special heartfelt thanks to my very own mitra, **Andrea Quigley**.

In the world of rugby, I have to praise my fellow veterans of **Barnes RFC,** who not only encouraged me to play but allowed me to proudly lead them onto the pitch for 3 whole seasons; so, special mention goes to the spine of that team — **Angus Graham**, **Richard Fenech**, **Jonny Speers** and **Jose Fernandez** — as well as to the many others who always enjoyed to play alongside, against, and also in the **Surrey County Mighty Oaks**, of which I had the pleasure to lead on the pitch, which was always enabled by the stalwart, **Brian Cassidy.**

In the development of **Mandala Leaders,** there are many who deserve credit for their huge contributions, starting with **Daniel Frohwein** who stood alongside me right at the beginning of the business, and indeed co-wrote some of the Mandala Leaders Process, and **Julie Clements,** who was my first guinea pig. Support followed from **Gregor & Asa Schill (Association of Business & Leadership Coaches)**; **Karen Tait**, who listened to early voice recordings of this book and tried to make sense of my words above the traffic noise; **Paul Farmer** of **Mentoris Group**, for encouragement and support; and **Simon Young** of **Limitless Digital**, who built me an invaluable network. I also want to acknowledge the friendship of **Michele Scataglini**, for his hospitality and dedication to his purpose.

The research I undertook at the start of this project showed me that there were unmet needs in many leaders, and that they were wanting more time to achieve their leadership potential, greater clarity on purpose, better promotion of legacy, and to grow in authenticity. I wanted to thank all those leaders who took part, and especially **Jo Moffatt** and **Edward Woyakovsky** for their in-depth contributions.

I also wanted to thank early clients and friends: **Andrew Thornton**, **Shanthy Lal**, **Parvin Nessa** and **Marco Amato** of **Budgens**, **Chris Notley** of **Chamberlain Career Management**, and the friendship and support of **James & Faye Fowler (KPMG)**, **Tom & Karina Milligan** (**Practice One**), and **Richard & Julie Bray** (**Chestnut Property Solutions**).

I have been delighted to spend the last year working with **3 Pillars Project**; we do amazing work to improve the wellbeing of young men in prisons, through rugby, education, and values, and I am delighted to have shared my enjoyment in this project with the CEO, **Mike Crofts**, as well as **Bex Norris**, **Will Mclay**, **Kazeem Olayinka**, and **Nick Hartley**, and with the generous support of **Nick Hamilton**.

It would be remiss of me not to thank those leaders who have influenced me over the years; some have shown me a positive way forward in my own leadership, and others have shown caution and how not to lead. But I am grateful to business people like **Richard Branson** and **Steve Jobs**, and politicians like **David Cameron**, **Boris Johnson**, **Theresa May**, **Nelson Mandela**, **Barak Obama**, and **Donald Trump**, and especially to **HM The Queen Elizabeth II** for her lifelong leadership and service.

Finally, my great thanks to the publishing team at Aaron Group, who have kindly published this book, starting with **Vishal Morjaria**, who was the first to suggest the idea of a book to me, **Naval Kumar**, **Chinmai Swamy, Rosie Duckworth**, and **Carla Van Wees. In addition Liz Ventrella and Lisa Browning who have edited and formatted the draft of this book.** Finally, of course, thanks to **Raymond Aaron**, for holding a unique space to allow me to write this book, and for his forthright drive and advice.

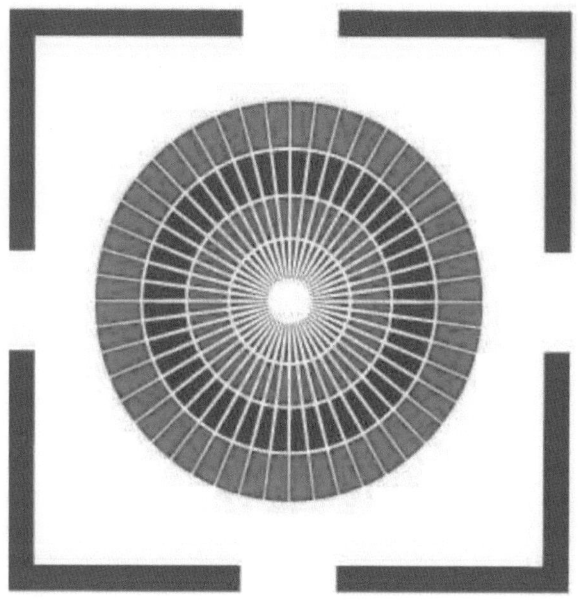

ZERO TO AUTHENTIC HERO

THE 7 KEY STEPS TO BECOME A <u>TRUE</u> LEADER

Introduction

"Authenticity is more than speaking; authenticity is also about doing. Every decision we make says something about who we are."
Simon Sinek, global bestselling author of *Start with Why: How Great Leaders Inspire Everyone to Take Action.*

<u>What Type of Leader Are You?</u>

You all will have experienced many different types of leadership. Many of them are in the public arena, such as politicians, military leaders, and historic leaders. Examples of these would be Sir Winton Churchill, George Washington, Barack Obama, Margaret Thatcher, and Donald Trump. Many of these leaders will have expressed certain leadership traits that can impact others in their own time, and even continue to impact those leaders who operate today.

Further to this, there are business leaders you may see—some are entrepreneurs, some are significant names such as Jack Welsh, Richard Branson, Bill Gates, or Steve Jobs—who all have their different leadership styles and, yes, all are successful in their own business and philanthropic fields.

You may admire sports leaders, like Franz Beckenbauer, Steve Yzerman, Jonny Wilkinson, Ricky Ponting, Michael Jordan, or Bobby Moore, who have excelled as both player and leader of their team, for many years.

It might be that you are more mindful of the business leaders we have experienced in the organisations where we have worked, both the good and the bad ones. Also, you may be inspired by your parents, or uncles or aunties, who have been running their own company; or, indeed, you may be in the family business.

You will have grown up with these types of leaders being in the news or discussed around the dinner table with our fathers, mothers, and families, and these will have had an impact on you and helped to shape your own leadership style as you have grown and experienced your personal and business life.

Different leadership manuals

There are many different types of leadership manuals that are popular best sellers and, in many organisations, the leaders will recommend various books to people they work with and think they should specialise in a particular leadership area.

If you were to take a look on Amazon and search for business books, you would be amazed that there are in excess of 100,000 entries to look at, and these are only the ones currently published through their website. This is even before I have taken into account the historic books, military history books, and political biographies that include leadership with many of these having influenced the current titles.

Yet many of these books teach specific skills, like time management or how to make better presentations. They are educational books to tell you how to do something better. Many of these books are bought because of a sense of obligation to improve one's particular skill, but they tend to sit on the bookcase without being fully read, understood, or implemented by the leader.

The other types of leadership books are the biographies or autobiographies from famous business, sports, and military leaders, which both tell their own story – often rags to riches – and how they did it. These books are sometimes a little self-serving and, whilst they may sometimes inspire others, they are also a source of income to supplement the otherwise wealthy lifestyle these leaders choose. There are not many readers of these books who can really connect to the same circumstances or challenges, and therefore follow this manual in order to make success for themselves.

How many of these books have you read, and taken on board new beliefs on how you should be a leader in your organisation?

Business courses

How many courses have you been on? Have these been days in the office, away-days, or even weeks in a beautiful country house hotel. Were they provided at the right time for your career, and did they teach you the skills you needed for your role?

In my experience, there tend to be three groups of people on work courses. The first group is those who are sent, as it's always provided to people in that role at that level or years' service, and sometimes this can be seen as a perk of the job.

The second group is those people who like to get away from work (and sometimes the family) for a few days.

The third group is where the business leaders have critically assessed the skills required by the individual, and have jointly found a great opportunity that is appropriate to fill that skill gap, and is provided at exactly the right time in the individual's career.

Unfortunately, the third group is usually the smallest proportion of those who the organisation spends money and time on providing a learning opportunity. This is often reflected on the business and personal benefits that are delivered back in the organisation.

The post course questionnaires at the end of the business break will usually give great feedback as everyone has had a relaxed break in a nice venue. In the last ten minutes of the program, the feedback given is quick and easy as the participants are already thinking about catching the train, driving along the motorway, or dinner back at home that evening.

It is very rare that a course seeks feedback three months later to see how the learning was implemented in the workplace, and even less rare that ongoing support is provided post course to ensure that the expected business and personal benefits are fully delivered.

What have you learnt, and what beliefs have you created from being on courses, and how have you continued to deliver the improved results to the organisation on a sustainable basis?

<u>Leaders Desire Authenticity</u>

In writing this book, I asked leaders to gift their wisdom to support a growing community of purpose-led leaders. The five key findings show a growing need for investment in time, removal of personal blockages, greater clarity, and developing authenticity. Leaders also told us that sharing their new wisdom is becoming increasingly important to help inspire others to follow a similar path.

1. The amount of time leaders spend on their personal development was surprising.

More than half of the leaders tell us that they plan to spend more than a week each year on their own personal development. However, only one quarter of the leaders make commitments for certain development opportunities, with the majority responding to ad hoc opportunities.

Michael Scattergood, a manager with accounting practice EY, says that “being seen to have a clear personal development plan inspires others.” This also leads us to believe that a better personal development strategy with planned activities would be beneficial to leaders, and would give them clearly defined goals to achieve and more time to prepare for their personal work.

2. Realise your leadership potential.

An overwhelming majority of leaders, seven out of ten in fact, say that there are old stories, subconscious beliefs, and lack of awareness, especially at times of conflict, which prevent them from realising their full potential as a leader.

They are asking for ways to have improved awareness of the issues, to understand them better, and find tools and processes to remove these blockages. “Mindfulness can be quite useful,” says Jo Moffatt, a well-regarded brand leader, but whilst this is certainly one well known tool, most leaders admit to not practicing this regularly or consistently.

A useful definition of personal development is spending time reflecting on yourself and learning more about what core beliefs you have, and from where these have developed. Then it’s about understanding better how these beliefs show up in your life.

Personal development is very different from technical business education or training.

3. Clarity is much sought after.

I was surprised that more than eight out of every ten leaders were seeking more clarity and courage in their leadership roles. Edward Woyakovsky, an entrepreneur specialising in hotel groups, says that a “much improved clarity in the business” is required by many leaders, and “this can support a better reputation both within the company and to the outside world.”

When it comes to clarity for leaders, the most critical issues, the leaders said, are around purpose, strategy, and vision. Second to these are the core values that appear in many businesses but remain poorly communicated and are not thus adopted.

4. Legacy needs greater promotion.

Only half of the leaders said they had time to develop a greater legacy and reputation. They told me that there is often too much focus on the day-to-day issues, which reduces the opportunity to look to the future.

“Create a legacy that other people adopt,” says financial services veteran, Steve Barningham, as this ensures the team is on the same page and working toward the same goals as the business leader.

5. Authentic leadership is a desire.

Two out of every three leaders showed a clear preference to be more authentic in their leadership style. This can only be achieved by having the right balance of (a) bringing greater awareness to the subconscious beliefs that often lead us into sub-optimal decision making, and (b) having clarity of purpose, which becomes the rallying cry that you can follow.

As Julie Clements, a coach to many women in the boardroom, puts it, "Authenticity is not something new, but showing your true colours in the workplace takes courage, and the world is ready for it now."

Summary

Leaders have told me that they spend more than one week each year on their own personal development to clear personal blockages that hold them back from being the best version of themselves that they can be. This allows them to have greater clarity, create a legacy, and act with authenticity in their leadership role, and this also plays out in their personal and family lives too.

<u>What is Authenticity?</u>

Authenticity is when you have a clear understanding of your beliefs and then choose which ones serve you, and discard the others. Often, you will then develop new beliefs that are your own and not those that you have inherited from others over the years.

It is when the subconscious beliefs that you picked up on your journey so far are brought forward into consciousness. It's the *unknown* unknowns being brought out and examined. Then, it's choosing whether these are true to you or the result of other's opinions of you.

By removing all these self-limiting sub-conscious beliefs, you can thus become truly authentic to your true self.

When you have been inspired by a leader, sports personality, military hero, or family member, you are likely to have taken on board some of their beliefs. These are the ways in which the leaders operate, work, treat other people, and succeed. But some of these beliefs may be self-limiting, barriers to action, and even destructive. It may be that they are positive and uplifting but need ever greater levels of perfection to achieve these, which is unsustainable.

Let me give you an example. How many times did you have a teacher tell you that you would never amount to anything? How does this one-off message swim around in your mind all the time? How does it either spur you on to prove them wrong or act as a blocker that proves them right?

Did you have a boss who always praised your work or only rewarded you with a bonus when you delivered something great? What did this mean to you, and what belief did you build as a result? Then, what happened when that boss moved on, or you delivered what you thought was great work and they disagreed? What was the impact on you then?

When you are driven by other people's beliefs, you tend to spend a lot of your time worrying about what is right and what is wrong—what you shouldn't be doing as opposed to what you haven't been doing. Sometimes you may have a desire to achieve and drive, and sell or deliver, and push hard, cut corners, take liberties, and annoy colleagues to close the deal.

Do you spend more time worrying about not being good enough, not achieving enough, or not delivering high enough quality? Do you then spend less time thinking that you are a fundamentally good person who is delivering well and making good progress?

The more time that you spend on worrying about the negatives, or reaching impossible highs in life, is time wasted. Compare this to time that could be used for positive, productive beliefs to create what it is that you need in your life—or that you want in your life—and to achieve the goals that you set personally.

Knowing who you are, what your beliefs are, and where they originated from, is moving towards authenticity. Authenticity starts from within, and only then can you start to inspire others or your whole organisation to practice authenticity too. This books starts with you.

What Does This Mean to Me?

I have spent 30 years in investment banking and management consultancy; as my career progressed in those environments, they became more and more dominated by alpha males and a few females driving towards crazy targets, delivering huge amounts of money to the organisations, and fighting over salary and bonuses.

Whilst this was beneficial in terms of remuneration and reward, for many years it also served to lead to patterns in terms of management style and choices, which were ultimately having a greater adverse impact on me than the positive impact of just the money.

I found that by enquiring deeply within that I was carrying a need to achieve, to deliver, and be proud, and though I had known this for many years, I had no tools with which to understand it properly, or techniques to lift the stress.

So, I continued in the vicious cycle of work hard, play hard, and earn hard, and this lead to hypertension, digestive disorders, fatigue, and muscular and skeletal pains, and left me tired and failing.

It took a number of major wakeup calls for me to see that there has to be a different approach, and I learnt that practising a more authentic leadership style was the person I wanted be. This includes having a greater awareness of my inner beliefs, and making choices each and every day as to how I want to act and what I say, to ensure that they are authentic to the person I choose to be.

This has led to a happier leadership approach and where I can actually take creativity and enjoyment through my leadership roles, as opposed to just crunching the numbers and getting the job done. This allows me more freedom with my time and gives me more opportunities to work smarter and with more exciting organisations. I also receive great benefits, which are not all financial, but they include creating better bonds and sustainable friendships, both inside and outside of the workplace.

Why Have I Written This Book?

I write this book to help you to understand yourself a little bit better—to take the first steps on the path of reflection, to become a truly authentic person and leader—and how that will have a huge beneficial impact on your life, the life of the people you lead, and the lives of the community you serve.

I have learnt much of my 30 years in business and my leadership qualifications from the University of Cranfield – School of Management, which taught me the basics, theory, and the strategy, but it is the experience that really has the greatest value.

In addition, I am a qualified business and leadership coach with the Association of Business and Leadership Coaches (ABLC), and the European Mentoring and Coaching Council (EMCC), and I want to share this experience with you now, and support you through this program.

I also founded Mandala Leaders, where there is a team of very experienced and qualified coaches, and through programs and executive coaching and leadership circles; I support leaders, and invite you to join this community of <u>true</u> leaders.

What Do You Do Next?

Having a clear purpose, strategy, and vision, and working each day in alignment with your core values, and communicating that with clarity—at least to yourself—are all going to lead to great success in a far easier way than is even imaginable to most people.

This means things get done, and results get delivered in an easier, friendly, and collaborative approach, without the need for dictating, driving, or shouting and screaming, and getting stressed about achieving the targets. Things happen in a remarkable way when there is a high energy and authentic approach by you, the leader.

The structure of this program is to support different learning styles, combining teaching through words, engaging through videos, and learning through interactive work exercises at every step. This encourages you to reflect on your own needs, to take ownership of your own process, and build yourself a plan.

Most importantly, every step of the program has a clear series of actions for you to take, and it is only by having the courage to take a first step, however small or large, to truly embed your new authentic self.

So, the question is, do you want to be the sum total of all those beliefs from others that have occurred to you over many years, or do you choose to be someone who is in control of your own beliefs, words, and actions, and chooses which bits and pieces of influence to collect and take forward in your life, leaving behind those that no longer serve you.

Do you simply want to be an unconscious leader, walking forward with a program of beliefs that have already been written for you by other people, or do you wish to bring them into consciousness and write your own program of beliefs that are actually authentic for you?

Each of the 7 steps will focus on a specific area to grow in authenticity. By going through each step, and completing the exercise at the end of each step, you to grow in authenticity.

I recommend that you approach each step with a 2-week interval between each one, which gives time for you to practice and embed what you have learnt in that step. The whole process then takes a maximum of 100 days and, at the end, you will build a plan for the next 100 days, to truly grow into deeper authenticity.

Do you have the courage to take a deep and personal look at yourself and your beliefs, and stick closely to the *Zero to Authentic Hero* program for 100 days?

Do you wish to become a <u>true</u> leader?

Notes

Step 1: Understanding Your Beliefs

"To be yourself in a world that is constantly trying to make you something else is the greatest accomplishment."
Ralph Waldo Emerson

The Two-Way Ripple Effect

Imagine you jump into the middle of a lake of still, cool water and, from the centre point of your impact, the water will ripple outwards in concentric circles. However, as the ripples move outwards from the still centre of the circle, it will also appear that the ripples flow back inwards towards you.

So, let's imagine that these concentric ripples coming to you at the centre of the lake reflect the subliminal messages that we see and hear from all of these leaders as we live our daily lives—the messages that we see on advertising hoardings, when we read magazines, and which are projected to us by the wider communities as to what the expectations are of leaders—the messages we hear from political, business, and sports leaders to whom we have an affinity.

The first ring represents the lessons we have learnt, or have been told through discipline from our parents and wider family. The next ring in is perhaps those messages and expectations that we hear from our community or religious upbringing, or perhaps from teachers during our school or college education. What was their leadership style, their ability, and what was their expectation of what a leader should look like?

The next ring in comprises of those leaders we see in businesses, those we have worked for, the good and the bad, and those that we have elsewhere in the businesses we follow, who will all have an impact on us either positively or negatively. The ring outside of that relates to our friends and how we see them as leaders, both in the businesses they work in and in our friendship group, or sport club or our social group. Who do we see as captain of the soccer, football, cricket, or hockey team? These rings coming back to the centre all represent beliefs of others that have been pushed onto you during your lifetime from a wide variety of sources. With you standing in the middle of all those ripples, I firmly believe that all of those beliefs have an inward flow and an effect upon you at the centre. Some of it will be picked up consciously, and much of it subconsciously, but they will all have an impact to mould and create the leader that is within you today.

That ripple effect, however, works the other way too, in that every belief will drive an action in word or deed that you take, and will have an impact on yourself—some could be amazingly positive and some very damaging. This could be what you do or what you say to yourself every day. What beliefs have you formed about yourself in the middle of this circle?

Also, whatever that belief you have in the centre of this circle will have a ripple effect back out again onto your family, partner, children, and parents. It will have an impact on your friends and social circle, the people you work with, and the people that work for you. Further, as those ripples flow, they will have a wider impact, maybe at a lower level but on the community, schools, religious institutions, and the wider population, as every belief you have drives a word or action, which will spread back through that ripple effect.

Leaders Need to Remove Old Beliefs

Earlier this summer, we asked leaders to gift their wisdom to support a growing community of purpose-led leaders. The key findings show a growing need for investment in time, removal of personal blockages, greater clarity, and developing authenticity. An overwhelming majority of leaders, seven out of ten in fact, say that there are old stories, subconscious beliefs, and lack of awareness, especially at times of conflict, which prevent them from realising their full potential as a leader.

They are asking for ways to have improved awareness of the issues, to understand them better, and find tools and processes to remove these blockages. “Mindfulness can be quite useful,” says Jo Moffatt, a well-regarded brand leader, but whilst this is certainly one well known tool, most leaders admit to not practicing this regularly or consistently.

Is it an Eagle or is it a Chicken?

There was once a farmer, in rural India, who kept chickens and sold them, and their eggs, in the local market to provide for his family. However, every day, the farmer would spend time watching a magnificent eagle flying overhead. He marvelled at the bird as it soared up and down the valley, then flying higher to dive down and catch its prey from the valley floor, or picking a fish straight out of the river.

One day, the farmer decided that he wanted to own an eagle; so, he searched where the eagle nested and saw it was on the very top of the mountain that overshadowed the valley. He spent a whole day climbing up the mountain and took an egg from the nest. When he returned to his farm, he placed the egg under one of his chickens so that it would care for it until it was time for the egg to hatch.

When the egg hatched and a tiny eagle popped out, the eagle found itself in a barn surrounded by chickens. It walked out into the farmyard and ate corn with the chickens. The eagle lived with the chickens, ate with the chickens, and slept with the chickens. So, is it an eagle or is it a chicken? A few months later, the original eagle flew over the farm and saw the young eagle scratching around in the dirt with the chickens. He called down to his son on the ground, “Fly up here with me my son.” The young eagle looked up and was amazed to see the incredible creature above him. The large eagle called again, “Soar up into the sky and fly alongside me.” However, the young eagle didn’t believe he could fly, and stayed on the ground.

The young eagle looked like his father in every way, but as he had lived with the chickens for so long, he had been subconsciously influenced by the chickens; so, he came to believe that he was a chicken, who could not fly.

What Are Your Beliefs?

When there is an action taking place, you will find that you will have a reaction. That initial action may be that somebody says something or does something. You then react positively or negatively, calmly or with anger, with joy or sorrow.

If you could understand more about how and why you react in a certain way, you could perhaps change that reaction to a more positive reaction. If you were able to do that on a regular basis, then we may have a more joyful life. If you were able to do that consistently, you may find that you are becoming more true to yourself and not to the beliefs that have been ingrained within you over the years.

So, I propose a structure that you should consider during your day, and the structure is something that brings greater awareness to your beliefs. It starts with an action, then a feeling, followed by a belief and, finally, by a reaction.

Action, Feeling, Belief, Reaction

Let me give you an example. Somebody comes up to you today, and says, "I really like the way you look." Your feeling might be, "Wow, that's amazing." But why do you feel like that? You probably feel that because of your belief, which has been ingrained over many years, of people telling you that you need to do things better, behave better, and work better and faster. You may have the ingrained belief that you are not good enough. So, therefore, when someone says you look great, you feel amazing because your belief is the opposite, and your reaction is, "Wow," and everyone has a good day.

A second example. If someone comes to a meeting and arrives 15 minutes late, you might be feeling frustrated, even angry, that this person is not valuing your time. Why is that? It might be that, as a child, you used to be influenced by your father, who always insisted on being everywhere on time, and maybe even 5 minutes early, and then when you were late, he would call out to everyone to announce that you were late, to shame you in order to try and teach you. But this now plays out in a belief that everyone has to be on time; otherwise, it is shameful. Therefore, when someone comes late to a meeting, the feeling is shame, because the belief is that you have to be on time. The outcome is a bad-tempered meeting.

Let me try a third example! From the moment the alarm clock rings, how do you react? Do you react with, "Great, another day!" and jump out of bed and make the most of it, or do you react with, "Great, I have to go to work; I have to do all these things. I want to go back to bed."

So, you get out of bed and go to the bathroom, and the water is cold for the shower. How do you react? Do you jump in a cold shower and get on with your day, or wait for it to warm up? Do you go and fix the boiler, or do you just have a good moan?

You go to breakfast and the kids are squabbling at the table. How do you react? Do you join in with them and make a game to gently move them from their squabble into something more positive, or do you just shout at them and tell them to shut up? How do you react?

It is a frosty morning and the car window is frosted over, and you don't have a scraper or de-icer to clear the windscreen to get to work. How do you react? Do you just improvise and find something else to scrape the window with, put your gloves on and get on with it, with a smile on your face, or do you moan, complain, curse at the weather and have a bad day? How do you react?

Or, perhaps you get the tube, and they are all delayed. Maybe someone has fallen or jumped under a train, which is going to put another 10 to 15 minutes on your journey to work. How do you react? Do you complain and get frustrated that you are going to be late, tapping your foot and getting angry with all the other passengers, or do you perhaps choose to have some compassion for the poor person who has taken such a dramatic step or were so confused with negative thoughts in their own mind?

All of these actions, and many, many more, are happening to you every day—in this case, even before you have arrived at work—and you get to choose how you react to them. You get to choose the kind of day you want; you get to have the option to be burdened by other peoples' actions because of your own beliefs, or you get the choice to let those go, and choose to react and create a new set of beliefs, reacting in a far more positive way, which feels better for you and is more natural or appropriate, or more enjoyable. It is not just beliefs that have been ingrained within you over the years; it is also your own choice or your own beliefs that have therefore made you truly authentic.

What are the impacts of these beliefs?

In the workplace, the same action, fear, belief, and reaction applies too.

All of a sudden, halfway through the year, the boss tells you that all your targets are being increased by 10%. How do you feel? Is it a sense of excitement or a sense of anger? Is that because your belief is that it is not fair, because fairness has been ingrained in you for many years, and that when fairness is agreed, it stays that way forever, and that it can never change or flex under any circumstances or influences from the outside. Just because it was fair when it was agreed doesn't make it fair six months later. And fair to whom—fair to you, fair to the other person, or other outside employees, or shareholders?

What is fair when the whole world is constantly changing? Perhaps fair has to change too? So, how do you choose to react? Do you come out in anger or sadness, or with a realisation that it has to be done and, therefore, face that challenge in a positive way?

What if someone produces a report for you, and the report simply doesn't cover the areas you wanted it to cover. How do you feel? Why do you feel that? Do you feel that because the person isn't good enough; do you think it is because they haven't tried very hard; do you think it's because they are an idiot?

Perhaps you weren't clear enough in your instruction to what your report should include. Was it because you didn't provide enough information to the person, or keep a check on them regularly during the report writing process to ensure that they were on track, and therefore taking your responsibility that the report was delivered properly. And now is it because you have to stand up in front of your boss and tell them that the report didn't do the job? Who do you blame—yourself, or the writer of the report?

Do you enjoy life, and work, or do you believe it's a burden?

Career-Limiting Beliefs

After a period of frustration and anxiety with his role, Michael Scattergood, a senior management consultant in EY's international development division, refocused on his career priorities, with support from Mandala Leaders. Through intensive coaching sessions, the executive has reappraised his job and his ambitions. Instead of pushing him towards a plan, Mandala Leaders helped him to make his own top-to-bottom appraisal of his role and communications with colleagues, while evaluating the wider impacts for government clients and citizens of his career-developing national health care programmes.

The challenge

Effective leadership coaching must gain a clear picture of the current state of play before seeking to make changes. Being a senior director of international development at management consultancy in EY, he has refocused on his career priorities, with support from Mandala Leaders, a consultancy dedicated to transforming the life of an individual and the communities they serve.

After years in a high-pressure job, delivering strategic plans for health systems to European governments, the management consultant was jaded. His energies were being drained by managing team capacity, workloads, and unrelenting deadlines. "I was worn down and edgy. I was reacting to specific criticisms of my work, from colleagues." He sought a fresh perspective on his priorities and wanted to reassess the value his work was bringing for himself and others.

The solution

In one-on-one coaching sessions with Mandala Leaders, the consultant was gently guided to reappraise his job and his ambitions. "There wasn't a right and wrong; we developed a clear, objective discussion of my feelings and my relationships with colleagues. We examined the way that I was collaborating and communicating with them," the executive explains.

In the first session, he was asked to articulate his beliefs about his role at EY, including the specific question of whether he was sufficiently valuing his own contribution. In striving hard to balance the delivery of complex projects, meeting divisional revenues and maintaining his team's capacity levels, was he registering only colleagues' criticism rather than their concern and support?

After getting the executive's perceptions of his day-to-day working, Mandala Leaders also helped him examine the bigger picture. The coaching session then asked the executive to define his career purpose, his strategy for realising it, and his vision of success, including the *forgotten* key questions: how were people benefiting from his work, and did he, himself, gain a sense of fulfilment from it?

In the final sessions, the executive was asked to state his personal values that defined his whole approach to leadership at work, and the likely legacy of his work for European countries.

Benefits

The sessions helped the EY management consultant to disentangle the confused priorities, perceptions, and impacts in a high-pressure job. He felt relieved and rebalanced afterwards— particularly as Mandala Leaders guided him to reappraise his role and his interactions with colleagues. The coaching identified the need for clear empathy and emotional intelligence when working with colleagues sharing unforgiving work pressures and deadlines.

The executive regained his perspective of his job—in particular, reflecting on the health care improvements that his consultancy work has brought to different countries over a period of years. He has learned to revalue his own skills and recognise the life-giving and quality of life benefits he and his EY colleagues have achieved for many millions of people across Europe, which arose from his ability to design national-level health programmes.

He has refocused his day-to-day skills: “I’ve realised the importance of better communication with colleagues, whatever the pressures. The coaching has given me a clearer perspective on my work ever since. I’ve committed to expressing myself more clearly, and phrasing things in ways that won’t be misconstrued by others.

The other side of improving my communication was being fairer to myself. In the workplace, one individual can place great importance on someone’s remarks when another puts little value on them. In a pressured workplace, it’s too easy to latch onto the wrong words—ones that can reinforce negative feelings a person harbours about oneself or others."

He added: "I have a better perspective on the long-term benefits that we have delivered across Europe's health systems, and what needs to be done in terms of leadership, collaborations, and communications, to get the right results in the future. I don't think I will be distracted or become worn down by internal politics like that again."

Reflection

In this step, you will have reflected your first thoughts on how the Two Way Ripple Effect has impacted on you over the years, and how you may have picked up some beliefs along the way. Reading about how others have reconsidered their own beliefs about their leadership style or their current position in life will have lead you to consider how you can perhaps create new beliefs.

The next step is to undertake the exercise over the following pages, which will really help bring home where some of your beliefs have come from and what the impact is; it will also give you an opportunity to reframe those beliefs in a different, positive way, which will lead to less stress, better connections, and more success than ever before.

In the following Step 2: Having a Clear Purpose – you will find the opportunity to understand perhaps the most important part of this process, which is where you will be able to gain clarity on your purpose, strategy, and vision, and then progress through the following steps to become a truly inspiring leader.

Understanding Your Beliefs – Exercise

Do you want to be your own person—authentic to what you want to believe going forward, as opposed to what you have been programmed to believe by all of those people that you have encountered in the past?

Take some time to reflect on what you have just read about the Two Way Ripple Effect and how you will have been influenced consciously or subconsciously by others.

The purpose of this exercise is to assist you to think more about these influences, and help increase your awareness of your beliefs.

Download the full size, full colour, ready to print worksheet, from ZeroToAuthenticHero.com and follow these instructions.

Part 1: Think of three leaders who may have influenced you, be they historical, military, sports, business leaders, or from your community or family. Let's call these people your *Leadership Heroes*. List them across Row 1.

Then, in the second row, insert where they are from: political, military, business, sports, community, family, etc. (Row 2)

Part 2: Work from top to bottom, one belief at a time, and complete Rows 3–6, answering the following questions:

What has the impact been on yourself in the past? (Row 3)

What has the impact been on others in the past? (Row 4)

What would you like the impact to be on yourself in the future? (Row 5)

What would you like the impact to be on others in the future? (Row 6)

Part 3: Then, choose what you want to do in the future: do you want to keep this belief, or leave it behind. You may want to keep the belief but drop the emotion or negative feeling that is associated with it. Make a decision of what you want from this moment forward. (Row 7).

UNDERSTANDING YOUR BELIEFS

		Leader 1 Winston Churchill	Leader 2 Richard Branson	Leader 3 Jonny Wilkinson
1.	Type of leader (Military, Business, Politics, Sports, Family)	Military / Politics	Business	Sport
2.	What is the belief you have inherited from this leader?	I have to be in control	Take a risk	I have to practice to become perfect
3.	What has the impact been on yourself in the past?	I have become stressed	I haven't taken enough risks and this has limited my potential	I have worked very hard to achieve
4.	What has the impact been on others in the past?	They feel controlled and run away	I may be considered boring	I have distanced myself form others I judge to be not good enough
5.	What would you like the impact to be on yourself in the future?	I want to have less tress	I want to achieve more	I want better connections with others
6.	What would you like the impact to be on others in the future?	I want to have better connections with others	I want them to join me in new ideas	I want them to join me
7.	What are you going to do differently going forward?	Accept that I cant control everything – allow others to control areas and I may learn form them	Take measured risks and try to bring others along with me	I need to judge less – accept myself and accept others as perfect in their own way.

Notes

Step 2: Having a Clear Purpose

"Exceptional organisations are led by a purpose,
a reason for being that transcends the everyday
and underlies everything they do."
Punit Renjen, Global CEO, Deloitte

In this step, you will find your fundamental reason for being. This will be your guide for your journey, and will help you every day and in every decision that you have to take. This will be supported by both a strategy and a vision, and these will, together, provide a clear route ahead.

Leaders Need a Clear Purpose

When we asked leaders to gift their wisdom, the key findings show a growing need for investment in time, removal of personal blockages, greater clarity, and developing authenticity.

We were surprised that more than eight out of every ten leaders were seeking more clarity and courage in their leadership roles. Edward Woyakovsky, an entrepreneur specialising in hotel groups, says that a "much improved clarity in the business" is required by many leaders, and this can support a better reputation, both within the company and to the outside world.

When it comes to clarity for leaders, we have been told that the most critical issues are around purpose, strategy, and vision. Second to these are values, which appear in many businesses but remain poorly communicated and, therefore, unclear.

Do We Make Rules or Do We Save Lives?

An example of this would be the Swedish road traffic agency. They are tasked in measuring the number of accidents on Sweden's roads, and to implement new laws, restrict speed levels, specify the width and brightness of white lines on the roads, and increase safety features in cars.

However, for many drivers, these are frustrating and annoying laws, which are either inconvenient or they reduce the enjoyment of driving, or indeed they are just simply odd. This means that The Swedish road traffic agency is having great difficulty encouraging drivers to engage with and observe these new regulations because their message was about safety, control, restrictions, and reducing the number of accidents.

The Swedish road traffic agency then decided they were going to have a clear purpose that drivers, road builders, car builders, and regulators could all buy into, engage with, and share the overall purpose of the organisation.

So, do we make rules or do we save lives? The new purpose of the agency was very simply to *save lives.* This made it very personal for the drivers who were also the customers of the car manufacturers, and they began to engage more with the new laws and, after a period of relatively stable accident numbers, these began to fall dramatically when this new purpose was clearly communicated to the market.

What is Purpose?

Purpose is your fundamental reason for being.

This is not what you achieve, or what you do, but why you do it. It's your *why*.

For a leader to be able to have real clarity on their purpose, they need to have a very short, memorable, higher purpose, which is over and above the day-to-day operational issues of the business and is even above the annual goals or objective of the company or organisation. The purpose is at a higher plain.

A clear purpose needs to be inspiring, motivating, and engaging, and only with this will employees, customers, suppliers, and all of the stakeholders, buy into what you are trying to achieve. The detail will follow, but this is a great place from which to lead.

Strategy

Once a clear purpose has been defined, the next stage is to build a strategy. The strategy is simply the actions you are going to take and what you are going to do. This will be a series of principals, overall activities of the organisation, and will be maybe five or six activities that will ensure everyone will drive in the same direction as the purpose. One of the strategies might be around customers; one might be around products; one might be around financial wealth of the business; and one might be about the employees or the other people the organisation seeks to serve.

The strategy of the business should flow automatically from the purpose. If you are going to be aligned with the purpose, what are the things you need to do to achieve that? What do the staff need to do? What do you need to provide for your customers? How do you treat your suppliers, and what other activities, products, services, or offerings do you need to create towards the overall purpose?

Vision

Once the strategy is clear, the final stage is to have a vision. Many companies create a vision or a mission without clearly defining the overall goal or how they are going to get there. The vision is what it will look like when you have delivered the strategy. How will you know you have got there, or how will you be able to measure that you are on the right track or making progress in the right direction? So, a vision needs to be measurable and specific, and then it needs to be defined by time.

This is getting closer to a SMART goal, or a series of goals within the organisation. SMART is a well-known set of criteria that the vision has to meet. The vision should be Specific, Measureable, Achievable, Realistic, and Time-bound.

Those businesses that set goals, without having the clear overall objective in mind, have goals that are short term and are often difficult to achieve, and lack motivation from employees. Once you have a clear purpose and strategy outlined, then the vision will fall into place and be far more engaging, and staff will be willing to participate.

Purpose, Strategy & Vision

So, when you have a clear purpose, strategy and vision, they should flow together, and the whole sentence or short paragraph should be memorable and inspiring. This then needs to be communicated to all of your stakeholders. First of all, you as the leader need to have real clarity in your mind and ensure that it covers your activities. Indeed, this will also help you to feel more aligned to the overall goals, and how you are going to achieve these.

However, if the purpose moves from alignment, from what you are currently doing, then there is the opportunity to really enquire as to whether you are currently doing the right thing. Just because you have always done it this way doesn't necessarily mean that you should continue in the future, when you have a clearly defined purpose.

Communication is key here; the message needs to be clear and engaging. It needs to be delivered from the heart and in a way that will really inspire action. It has to be carried through with an overriding passion.

One of the other benefits of having a clear purpose, strategy, and vision is that it is a real aid to making difficult decisions. When there is a question of why you are doing something—whether you should try something new, or why you continue to do what we have done for years, or whether we should invest money in a new project or factory, or whether we should look at different countries or new products—these are often considered by business plans, strategies, action plans, and financing.

These decisions should always be compared to your purpose. Does it serve the overall purpose of what you do? Is it aligned to your strategy? Will it help you achieve your vision to support more people or to do it more quickly? If the answer to these questions is no, then you should be really careful before spending money or allowing the continued spend of money when it is not aligned with the agreed purpose, strategy and vision.

It is most important, however, that the clearly communicated purpose, strategy, and vision is not just put out there and then forgotten. It is the responsibility of the leader to keep it alive, to utilise it each and every day, and to talk openly and passionately to others about it and how you are progressing. Most importantly, though, it's not just talking about purpose but actually living it in each and every action you take.

Purpose Brings People Together

Two busy doctor's practices in Yorkshire had tried to merge two years ago, and bringing the teams of partners and staff together had failed, leading to the whole merger being abandoned. Some partners felt that they were not being heard and that their own individual needs were being ignored by others.

Working with the *Zero to Authentic Hero* program, all of the partners worked together—and learnt much more about each other—to develop their purpose, strategy, and vision, which aligned their needs, along with those of their staff and patients, and successfully kicked off the integration process.

A diverse group of partners had very different expectations from the previous merger process, with some seeking an exit to retirement, some wanting to grow into leading roles, and some others simply wanting to continue to deliver great service to their patients. The practice could also use the merger to deliver significant process changes and cost saving initiatives, which would simplify processes for staff, improve the patient experience, and deliver a greater return to the partners.

In some ways, the differing views of the partners, and challenges of both merger and changing processes, became overwhelming, with various individuals focused on *"what does it mean to me?"* Could the partners find a new approach to bring together their individual needs, along with those of the wider staff, and how they could outline the benefits to their patients?

Solution

Mandala Leaders' founder, Nick Bradley, devised an intensive, one-day program for the partners from both practices, and led them through a series of exercises to develop a shared purpose, strategy, and vision.

Partner, Dr. Nicole Nunn, said, "People who are involved in creative teams will scatter down words to start with, and this worked well for these people." She continued, "People trusted in Nick, and his approach was required to encourage people to join the exercises, some of which were uncomfortable."

Dr. Priya Reddy added, "Letting the quiet people talk, and minimising the impact of the dominant people in the group, was valuable; encouraging the group to build their own trust and understanding was really good."

The team also developed a clear strategy and vision so that they knew what steps they needed to take going forward, and had a clear and shared idea of what the combined practice would look like for all stakeholders.

Benefits

The team now have a clear purpose, strategy, and vision, which all of the staff can buy into, and which is a benefit to the 14,000 patients in the town. This brought the teams together and gave them common ground from which to move forward.

Dr. Tom Milligan shared his experience, saying, "The work was good, but only on later reflection did I realise that this was actually a team-building process. I'm head and shoulders ahead of where I would have been without it, and I'm so glad we have acknowledgement of the past and have created a purpose to work together. This will prevent us from repeating previous mistakes.

Reflection

This step demonstrates the real benefits of having a clear purpose, strategy, and vision, and how it can be a guiding light for you as a leader. Whether this is for yourself, your team, or organisation, it carries great value in all areas. Your purpose, strategy, and vision will be your approach to leading, your key actions and deliverables, and view of success.

The following few pages show the purpose process; this is your opportunity to work out your own purpose, strategy, and vision, and will help and support you to gain real clarity, as well as to communicate this and keep accountable to it.

The strategy element may need some more work, and there are many different models to use; your personal preference should be the deciding factor of how to approach this. However, with this program, you will find a basic level of strategy, which is a great place from where to start.

I suggest that you work this through and spend a little time getting used to it. Practice it on others, and test drive it before you finalise your work. Try it on for size for a couple of weeks before you launch to a wider group, so that you know that not only is it right for you but that it feels right too.

In the following Step 3: Living your core values – you will learn your core values, which is the way to approach delivery of your purpose and many of the other steps in the book; by the end of this step, you will have clarity on how to live in alignment with these core values.

Having a Clear Purpose – Exercise

Purpose – this is your WHY. It's your reason for being, for doing, for what you are giving to others. It's big and bold and fearless. It can be broad and powerful and inspiring. It will also connect with others.

Strategy – This is your WHAT. What will you do, how will you do it, and who will do it? What resources are required? Who are you giving to, and what is the benefit you and they will receive?

Vision – What will this LOOK like? How much money will you make, how many others will you serve, how big will you be, what will others say about you, and what the press say about you? This should be SMART.

The worksheets in the pages that follow are the examples used by the NHS Yorkshire practice I shared earlier in this step, but you can download the full size, full colour, ready to print worksheet from ZeroToAuthenticHero.com and follow these instructions:

Part 1: List all of the descriptors for yourself. Split these between Emotional and Rational descriptors. These are different descriptors and have different thoughts and emotions attached to them; some are emotional and some are rational. When you have completed this list, try and reduce it to a maximum of eight items on each side.

Part 2: Add to each of these descriptors the reason WHY they are so important. This will prompt the reason why each of these descriptors are vital for you.

Part 3: Narrow down both the Emotional and Rational descriptors into 3–5 of each. There may be some duplication or one can be covered by another, and these can be streamlined to the most important descriptors. Aim to have four rational and four emotional.

Part 4: Talk about the key elements of each of the chosen descriptors. List out what it is, what your beliefs about it are, and why you are doing it. Copy the *whys* onto a separate piece of paper, and work through the most resounding words. These are the key reasons to do something.

Create a form of words in one sentence that explains the key *whys.* Elevate these *whys* to a higher level, and escalate them again and again until they become global, huge, and life-changing in their nature. This will become your purpose.

Part 5: Set up a communication plan – who do you need to communicate this to, and how are you going to totally embed the purpose, strategy, and vision into your organisation. You may wish to test drive them with a focus group. Perhaps list them in a way where a mnemonic, using the first letters, with make them easier to remember.

Create an action plan, test the purpose, strategy, and vision, and communicate and embed them into the culture.

Part 6: Have a daily check-in. Each morning, check in with yourself about your purpose. Connect with this, and remind yourself of its origin and meaning.

Then, check in with others and ensure that you are living the purpose, and constantly and consistently talking about it and using it, especially where there are areas of conflict.

HAVING A CLEAR PURPOSE (1)

Emotional Descriptor	Why?	Rational Descriptor	Why?
Happy / Grateful	For well-being and being more productive	Efficient	Make work easier and manageable. Benefit of patients. Job satisfaction
Safe	Critical to the business and reputational issues.	Profitable	
Fearless		Safe for patients	
Transparent (value)		Quality	Make more impact on patients' life. Attract more people
Respectful		Common understanding	
Looking after		Teaming	
Family friendly	Happy, looking after each other.	Entrepreneurial	
Loyal		Innovative	Reduce workload. Move with time. Doctor as a teacher.
Acceptance (value)		Leading by example	
Informal		Pioneering	

HAVING A CLEAR PURPOSE (2)

Emotional Descriptor	Why?	Rational Descriptor	Why?
Inclusive		Risk taking	
Engaged		Looking after staff	
Approachable		Professional	
People focused	Safety: we are not vets	Focused	
		Outcome oriented	
		Business like	
		Flexibility and endurance	To manage change and stay in business
		Delegation	
		Flat organization	
		Engaged	

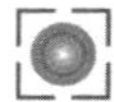

HAVING A CLEAR PURPOSE (3)

Emotional Descriptor	Why?	Rational Descriptor	Why?
		Training and developing people	
		Rewarding people	
		Autonomy	
		Complexity of tasks	
		Setting boundaries	
		Looking after	
		Self-development	
		Grateful/Happy	Work-life balance. Emotional well being

HAVING A CLEAR PURPOSE (SHORT LIST)

Emotional Descriptor	Why?	Rational Descriptor	Why?
Happy / Grateful	Well-being. Being more productive	Efficient	Make work easier and manageable. Benefit of patients. Job satisfaction
Safe	Critical to the business, reputational	Quality	Make more impact on patient's life. Attract more people.
Family friendly	Happy, looking after each other	Innovative	Reduce workload. Adapt to trends. Doctor as a teacher. Promote health.
People focused	Safety – not vets	Flexibility and endurance	To manage change To stay in business
		Grateful/Happy	Work-life balance. Emotional well being

HAVING A CLEAR PURPOSE

Purpose – this is your WHY. It's your reason for being, for doing, for what you are giving to others. Its big and bold and fearless. It can be broad and powerful and inspiring. It will connect employees, customers, investors and stakeholders. We are a friendly family practice, striving to deliver safe high quality services in more innovative ways.
Strategy – This is your WHAT. What will you do, how will you do it and who will do it. What resources are required. Who are you giving this to (your customers) and what is the benefit they receive. Together we will create a collaborative partnership to improve patient journey through developing processes and systems by building on our strengths and better utilising our shared resources.
Vision – What will this LOOK like. How much money will you make, how many customers will you serve, how big will you be, what will your customers say about you, what the press say about you. This should be SMART. We will be a GP Led practice which by 2022 will deliver: Friends and Family and NHS Survey scores to 95% Deliver local health scores growth by 3% Significant events and complaints reduced by 5% Improve staff satisfaction scores by 10%

HAVING A CLEAR PURPOSE - PLAN

Goal	Implement	Communicate	Live
4			
3			
2			
1			
Start			

Accountability Process:

Notes

Step 3: Living Your Core Values

"The quality of our relationships has very little to do with what we do, and a lot to do with how and why we do it."
Jesper Juul – Founder of FamilyLab

We have talked about purpose, strategy, and vision—why, what, and what it looks like—in the previous step. Here, we are going to talk about an additional area: values or, indeed, the *how* you go about living your life.

Most leaders talk about their own values, although how many actually communicate these clearly, ensuring they are being lived, and consistently living them themselves. All too often, the values of the leader are not communicated; they are not clear for others, and they very quickly get lost, forgotten, or overridden by new pressing challenges.

So, I believe that a handful of clear and concise values are needed to be the way in which you will live your purpose and how you interact with yourself and others. These need to be lived day in and day out, which is much more likely to help them stick. This leads to better results and less stress for the leader. However, you may be surprised to find that values also create value.

Values Create Value

Does it really matter what list of values a company ends up with, as long as they can present *something* to the world? This was one of the questions posed by a team at INSEAD, which is rated the number 1 global business school by the *Financial Times.*

They looked at Fortune 100 firms, from 2005 to 2008, to determine which values were espoused on their corporate websites; whether they differed from companies within the same industry, and how they compared to the common values of other Fortune 100 companies. They also examined whether any of this was correlated with actual (financial) performance. Additionally, they were interested in seeing whether companies changed their values over a period of time, and whether this had any effect on performance.

What the INSEAD team found was that, of the 32 values listed, there was not an enormous difference expressed across industries, but when companies *did* differentiate themselves from their industry peers, it had a positive effect on their firm's performance: the implication being that when actively seeking some uniqueness from the industry norm, even in how they shape their cultures, the firms in question outperformed others in their industry.

What seems to matter, too, is that companies who show more dynamism around their values—those that change them over time—outperform firms who kept theirs stable. The team would argue that these firms are seen to be more actively engaged in a conversation about *who* they are, what their culture is, and in which direction they are taking their business, precisely because they are wrestling with their organisational culture, rigorously defining and articulating it.

In effect, *tweaking* their values shows that these companies are actively trying to reform and improve themselves, which we believe is connected to their financial performance.

Should the Monk Carry the Woman?

There were two monks walking back from the local market town to their monastery one afternoon, having been shopping for food. On their journey, they came to a river where they could usually walk across a shallow stretch of water, but the recent rain had made the river swollen and, instead of the water coming to the monks' ankles, it appeared to be waist deep.

There was a woman standing on the bank of the river, and she was crying. The first monk went to ask her what was wrong, and she said that she would be unable to cross the deep river and get home to her two young children who were expecting her to cook them dinner.

This created a problem, as whilst the monks were tall and strong enough to wade through the water, the woman was obviously not willing to take this risk. There was no bridge, boat, or other way around the river. The older monk suggested that he carry the woman on his back and wade through the river to carry her safely to the other side. The younger monk chastised the older one, saying, "We can't help this woman; our religious order prevents us from touching a woman." The older monk ignored his younger friend and carried the woman on his back across the water, and safely placed her down on the other side so that she could continue her journey in order to provide food for her family.

So, why did the monk carry the woman? The monks continued their journey and, a few miles later, when they were finally approaching their monastery, the younger monk said that he was still troubled by his older colleague's action in breaking their religious code.

The older monk responded by saying that he had put the woman down after they had crossed the river, and it was the younger monk was the one still carrying her. He explained that whilst the younger monk was learning his religious practice, he was actually living his, and one of the core values of their teaching was to help others. This is what he had done by carrying the woman so that she could feed her family.

Which Values to Choose

There are many values to choose from—indeed, almost any can suit. Therefore, it can be a very difficult process to refine these into a cohesive and memorable list. So, let's start with some rules:

- Start with a long list of values, and rationalise these to just a handful.

- Document what the value means to you and how you would live in alignment with it.

- Create a plan about how to communicate the values and what they mean.

- Maintain alignment with the values—live the values—and check in daily that they are being lived.

When I founded the business and sports leadership coaching organisation, Mandala Leaders, I wanted to have an agreed set of values, which would be the guiding principles by which I led and the team worked together, and also the approach we would take to all of the clients.

I worked through the Values Process, which you will find on the following pages, and I included the following four values into the process; and even though I worked through the whole process, it was these values that came out the other end.

I don't want to pre-empt your own values; it's important that you find ones that work for you—ones you can step into and feel authentic, and which you can live every day—as any individual or organisation can choose any of their own values using this process.

However, I was inspired by the following four values, which I use both personally and in my leadership coaching business. These values are Personal Responsibility, Personal Integrity, Equal Dignity, and Authenticity. I have learnt that there are four core values, and I firmly believe that these are the only values you will ever need. It may be that you choose a couple more to represent yourself or your organisation, but these core values cover the bases.

Personal Responsibility

This is taking ownership for your thoughts, feelings, actions, and reactions. It is also accepting the consequences that follow from how you speak and act with others in your personal and professional life.

Personal Responsibility is a willingness to look at oneself rather than at others and pointing a finger of blame. It includes taking responsibility for our own mistakes, and rectifying these.

Personal Integrity

The connection between our head and our heart: it can be very easy to lose this connection to our moral compass when we are consumed with everyday problems, but a great way to connect to your personal integrity is to pause for a moment and simply ask, "How do I feel about this?" as well as "What do I think about this?"

Personal Integrity is the voice of conscience; how many times would things have turned out differently if you had just stopped to ask yourself this question? Many people worry more about what others will think of them rather than what they feel about themselves.

Equal Dignity

We all know about treating others as we would wish to be treated ourselves, but how often do we treat ourselves as we would wish to be treated by others? We can treat others with equal dignity even if we are angry, and nothing prevents us from doing this unless we are unable to treat ourselves with equal dignity too.

So, try not to judge others or yourself unfairly, and don't talk down to, lecture, vote down, label, or make fun of others or yourself. Treat others and yourself with equal dignity.

Authenticity

Authenticity is being real with yourself and speaking your truth. It's communicating as clearly and honestly as you can, without using sarcasm, criticism, or manipulation to get your point across. It's being aware of your beliefs and how they are playing out in any given scenario.

Sometimes it is as easy as simply asking someone to move rather than telling them that they are in your way. This may seem obvious, but pointing out somebody's mistake is not asking them to do it differently. Speaking clearly and honestly avoids confusion, conflict, and chaos.

Reflection

In this step, you will have seen how to develop a set of values for you to live with, and create a plan around how to choose these, communicate these, and indeed live by them. These will be your moral compass, your guide how to behave, and how to treat yourself.

The values process that follows will lead you to create your own set of values and a plan to live with them, and I encourage you to try this now. Do please ensure that you find values that are authentic to you, and create an accountability process with support to help you ensure that you live with these.

In the following Step 4: Improving your skill set – will help you to uncover a key area where authenticity is regularly tested. By improving your skill set, you will take away excuses and opportunity to behave in a non-authentic manner and, therefore, grow in authenticity. This will also engage you better with others in your organisation, inspire others to take similar action, and improve the overall skill level of your team.

Living Your Core Values – Exercise

Using the exercise sheets, follow this process, but remember the rules we discussed earlier.

1. Start with a long list of values, and rationalise these to just a handful.

2. Document what the value means to you and how you would live in alignment with it.

3. Create a plan about how to communicate the values and what they mean.

4. Maintain alignment with the values—live the values—and check in daily that they are being lived.

The worksheets on the following pages are from when I created Mandala Leaders and worked through the values I wanted to have in the business. You can download the full size, full colour, ready to print worksheet from ZeroToAuthenticHero.com and follow these instructions:

Part 1: Take a look at the list of values (Page 1 and 2) where there are already more than sixty values listed, and they include the four values of Personal Responsibility, Personal Integrity, Equal Dignity, and Authenticity. Some of these may work for you, and you may prefer sector specific or other preferences.

You may wish to cut out each of the values and work in a clear space, and place them into 3 piles: Yes, Maybe, and No. In the Yes pile, place those values that shout out to you; in the No pile, place those that don't connect; and for the few that you can't decide, the Maybe pile is the place for these.

Then, discard the Maybe and No piles. This is a challenge for some people as it takes real conviction and belief in the Yes pile; but without these attributes, you are unlikely to ever live the values that you choose!!!

Part 2: Take the Yes pile and go through the same exercise again. Place these values into three piles: Yes, Maybe, and No. In the Yes pile, place those values that shout out to you; in the No pile, place those that don't connect, and for the few that you can't decide, the Maybe pile is the place for these. This stage should bring the number you have chosen down to around 10–12.

Part 3: Copy this shortlist of values across to sheet 3. Take a closer look at these and see if any are ambiguous, unclear, or have potential differing meanings. Record what the values mean to you, and weed out those that do not have a clear meaning that is easily remembered.

Part 4: Finally, rationalise the list to 4 values. There are times where 5 or 6 work better, but ensure that they work together and can be easily memorised and understood. Copy these values and a very short summary of their meaning to the values wheel on sheet 4. These are your values!!!

Part 5: Set up a communication plan – who do you need to communicate these to, and how are you going to totally embed them into your organisation? You may wish to test drive them with a focus group. Perhaps list them in a way where a mnemonic, using the first letters, will make them easier to remember.

Create an action plan, test the values, communicate, and embed them into the culture.

Part 6: Have a daily check-in. Each morning, check in with yourself about your values. List them to yourself, along with their meaning. When I first did this exercise, I had a practice of writing them on my arm each morning until I had memorised them.

Then, check in with others in your organisation and ensure that they are living the values and constantly and consistently talking about them and using them, especially where there are areas of conflict.

Create an accountability process. This is a way for you to ask for help from another person and check in with them on a regular basis. Using clear communication, ask for their support and a structured approach, without excuse or blame; this is an incredibly powerful process to help keep you on track.

LIVING YOUR CORE VALUES (1)

Adventure	Competition	Environment	Helping Others	Knowledge
Artistic work	Conserve resources	Ethics	Impact	Leadership
Authority	Contact with people	Excellence	Improvisation	Learning
Authenticity	Contribution	Exciting activities	In the spotlight	Love
Being expert	Control	Fairness	Independence	Loyalty
Calm	Cooperation	Feedback	Influence	Meaning
Challenge	Creativity	Fellowship	Ingenuity	Mistakes possible
Collaboration	Determination	Freedom	Intellectual work	Money
Community benefit	Diversity	Gain	Involvement	Order
Compassion	Equal Dignity	Harmony	Joy	Organization

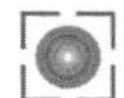

LIVING YOUR CORE VALUES (2)

Participation	Respect	Take decisions		
Personal Growth	Responsibility	Take risks		
Personal Integrity	Results	Team work		
Personal Responsibility	Solidarity	Tempo		
Persuade	Stability	Time Freedom		
Power	Stake	Truth		
Privacy	Status	Variety		
Profit	Structure	Well paid		
Purpose	Success	Working alone		
Quality	Sustainability			

LIVING YOUR CORE VALUES - SHORTLIST

Authority	Support
Contribution	Community
Authenticity	Leadership
Stability	Equal Dignity
Contact with people	Time Freedom
Personal Responsibility	Influencing
Impact	Personal Integrity

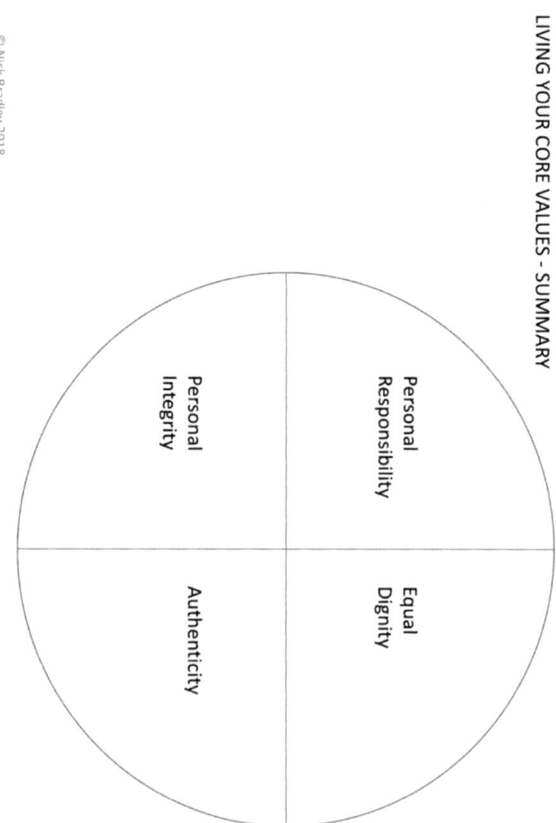
LIVING YOUR CORE VALUES - SUMMARY
Personal Responsibility
Equal Dignity
Personal Integrity
Authenticity
© Nick Bradley 2018

LIVING YOUR CORE VALUES - PLAN

Goal / **Week**	Measure living values by 360 degree feedback report	Introduce to all of team	Implement into coaching program
4	Practice values with all stakeholders	Create team work day to implement these and create working examples / examples	Write client facing process and worksheets
3	Work through examples with clients	Obtain feedback from team and adapt as necessary	Work through client feedback and adapt process if necessary
2	Work through examples in the office	Ask team to test drive new values for a week	Ask clients for feedback on process and outcomes
1	Work through examples at home	Work through values process with team to agree core values	Test drive process with 3 clients
Start	Values chosen	Values chosen	Written values process

Accountability Process: Weekly check-in with my coach

Notes

Notes

Step 4: Improving Your Skill Set

"The growth and development of people is the highest calling of leadership."
Harvey S. Firestone, Firestone Tire Company

In this step, you will come to see how valuable it is to fully understand your current skill set, as well as how to create a plan to improve this. In addition, there is an exercise to complete for you to reflect on how satisfied you are with your own skills, and then take action to improve.

Many leaders like you have come up through the ranks of an organisation and have become quite adept at handling the day-to-day tasks required in a role. You know either how to engage your customers, how to create product, how to market the service, how to use cost effective procurement, or whatever it is that you have been doing in the role.

However, when you step into a new leadership role, especially when it's your first in the business or organisation, the skill set that is required becomes very different. The people within the team will come to you, their leader, with an expectation that you can do the new job that you do.

This is not always the most beneficial way to create a leader. The skill set required by you, as the leader, is somewhat different to the skill set to some actually doing the role in the team. In addition to having a fundamental knowledge of what the team does, you can add value whilst also having a full set of leadership skills.

Setting strategy, for example, is one skill set that will benefit your leadership but is not necessary within the team itself. Another may be a basic knowledge of financial accounting and reporting to ensure that you know that the team's performance is being reported properly, and that both the revenues and costs are being measured in an appropriate manner.

People management is possibly a new skill that you require. As you progress to higher levels of leadership within the organisation, then greater skills regarding people management and coaching grow in importance.

There is also a skill of stakeholder management within the organisation, with you having greater responsibility for connections inside of the organisation, including finance, human resources, distribution, produce development, sales, etc.

In addition, there are more important relationships for you to manage with external stakeholders, like suppliers, customers, finance providers, advisors, interest groups, lobbying bodies, trade organisations and shareholders. The skills you require to manage a diverse set of stakeholders is very different to those skills required when you are within the team.

Here is one really important point: whilst the team members may have some great expectation that you are the new incumbent in the leader's chair, and you are fully versed in these skills, the reality is the opposite. These skills need to be learned and practiced in order for you to become fully competent in them. What is true, however, is that the leadership group, who made the decision to give you that leadership role, believe that you have the ability to learn and practice these skills.

Why Did the Elephant Stay by the Tree?

A young elephant was bought at market and taken back to its place of work by the new owner.

The owner tied the young animal to a tree and left it there overnight, where it struggled and pulled at the rope, trying to free itself to find its way back to its mother. Day after day, the elephant tried to fight its way out of its prison, and day after day, it failed to release itself.

Over the next few long days, weeks, and months, the elephant walked around and around the tree and grew increasingly frustrated at its plight. Each day, it would be taken to the forest, which had once been home, to carry logs that had been cut from the trees. Every night, the elephant was returned to the tree where it was once again tied up.

Three years later, the elephant was still being worked hard in the forest each day, and returned to be tied to the tree each evening. However, the elephant no longer tried to escape but was docile and accepting, even though it had now grown to such a size that it could easily wrap its trunk around the tree's trunk and tear it out of the earth.

So, why did the elephant stay by the tree? The elephant had tried again and again to free itself when it was younger but had grown the belief that it was unable to do so. However, as it grew, it gained new skills of size and strength, and these skills could easily have been applied to smash the tree, but it did not believe that it was able to do so.

Which Skills Need Improving?

I'm going to ask you to step outside of your role for a short time, to take a mental break from the day-to-day work, to find a place where you can really reflect, without the pressure of the role. This place may be home; it may be the gym or on a country walk. It may be after yoga or meditation.

Then, I will ask you to think clearly about the top eight skills that are required to do that job. It may be that the job description includes a list of skills that are required or expected by the organisation. This is always a good starting point to assess the skills of the role; but, in addition to this, you may have visibility on one or two additional skills that are more relevant to that particular role, and less so to other peer group roles across the organisation. When you step out of the role, you can critically assess the skills required for the role more carefully, and select the top eight skills required to ensure that these are valid.

It may be that you choose to discuss this with your superiors or peers within the organisation; and in large organisations, the HR department will also make a valid contribution to this discussion. Once you have got clarity on the eight skills for the role, then you have to truly critically assess how clear you are with your own skill set. This is not really about the judgement of being good enough or having enough experience or technical knowledge; this is more of an assessment of your satisfaction with your own set of skills. This is where you have to look inside yourself and be honest, and this helps you move further towards authenticity. Ask yourself: how satisfied am I with my level of this skill?

If you have a belief that you have to be good at sales, for example, because this has been dripped into you over the many years, then you may feel you are good at sales, or you may feel you are not good enough—but, actually, what levels of sales skills are required within your particular role? I will then ask you to score your level of satisfaction against those skills. This is a challenging process and may take some time.

There are other ways to validate your own satisfaction levels, including use of feedback through 360 degree feedback surveys, or selecting a group of trusted individuals to have a face to face conversation with. If you are a courageous leader, then you may also wish to seek feedback from outside the organisation; in particular, from the key stakeholders.

This will give you a really clear view of the satisfaction level, and it is very important to ensure that when others are being asked to contribute to this, it is very much a satisfaction- based question and not a judgement of the good or otherwise. You will have a really clear view of the skills that may need to be improved.

A truly authentic leader will have a real clarity on their own skills, and will then investigate what the impact is on themselves, and the team, of having skills where they are not satisfied. A good leader will acknowledge this and take time to improve those skills by seeking further education, knowledge, training, or experience in these particular areas.

I have found that leaders who ignore their skill set, or do not make solid visible progress towards growing their satisfaction with their skill set, tend to be less comfortable in their role, are less able to make strong decisions, and receive less respect from their team.

But what a great sign this is to the rest of the team that you are showing true leadership by being honest with yourself and looking to improve your abilities, not only for your own benefit but for the benefit of the overall team. This will also encourage team members to actively grow their own skills sets that are relevant to their roles. It is only by being honest with yourself that you can make progress by improving your own skills, improving your relationship with others, and inspiring your team to follow your example.

Skills in the Workplace

Thornton Budgens' chief financial officer, Shanthy Lal, has successfully refocused her communications with board members and shop floor colleagues alike, through a 100-day leadership coaching programme with Mandala Leaders.

Shanthy has now made her voice heard, assumed board-level decisions for the franchise's North London store, is intervening more effectively in cases of staff disagreement, and is motivating colleagues with a greater insight, and to greater effect.

This career breakthrough came through one-on-one coaching sessions with Mandala Leaders, which placed the emphasis firmly on her to take responsibility for transforming her role and the way she was perceived.

Situation

An executive assuming a company leadership role, when coming from a purely accounting background, can face some surprising and delicate hurdles. After helping build profitable operations at Thornton Budgens' Belsize Park franchise in North London, chief financial officer, Shanthy Lal, wanted to take on board-level responsibilities. But despite her lasting contribution, franchise owner, Andrew Thornton, wanted Shanthy to assume a more visible, senior role, and apply her know-how in the business to make the breakthrough to official board-level responsibilities, and lead the store's development.

In some ways, her growing role and a strong work ethic—clearly aligned with Thornton Budgens' community-focused, problem-solving ethos—was holding her back. Alongside core budgeting and forecasting duties, Shanthy had taken responsibility for a lot of staff-related procedural and compliance work over time. But being the franchise's recognised *fixer* only served to obscure colleagues' perceptions of her: what was her remit? It also made senior executives question if she had the high-level decision-making ability and the soft skills to take on a director-level post. Could Shanthy advocate a new corporate strategy to sceptical board members while continuing with day-to-day operations?

Solution

Andrew Thornton and co-directors invested in individual coaching, turned to Mandala Leaders, a consultancy dedicated to transforming the life of individuals and the communities they serve, for assistance. Mandala Leaders' founder, Nick Bradley, devised an intensive 100-day leadership coaching programme for Shanthy to reframe and then meet her challenge.

One-to-one sessions between Nick and Shanthy placed the onus on her to outline the goal and show the necessary qualities to step up a level. This self-directed rethink was hard but rewarding: "Nick didn't tell me what I should do; he made me prioritise," Shanthy explains. "He folded his arms and waited at several points; I knew I had to own the changes for them to really happen."

Through this definition exercise, Shanthy identified three specific hurdles: better communicating her contributions and ideas in board meetings, dealing with staff disagreements more efficiently, and communicating more effectively, day-by-day, with senior colleagues and shop floor staff alike.

Shanthy made subtle but far-reaching changes as a result. “I enforced board decisions more rigorously. I prepared financial reports before meetings, which justified my ideas. By making these changes, I gained in authority. By circulating the right information, I had the arguments to make my case.”

Shanthy also changed her approach to dispute resolution. “Before, when there were staff tensions, I used to get involved in many things, even down to email disagreements; now, I intervene purely to get the job done, and I don’t get drawn into the details.”

Shanthy also became more selective in her interventions with colleagues, and demonstrated greater empathy with the staff as a whole. “Before, I invested too much effort in trying to resolve disagreements that were essentially personality clashes,” she explains. “I accept other people’s differences more readily now, and I can actually help more colleagues with their jobs.”

Benefits

Shanthy’s confidence—at board level and beyond—has grown, and her ideas are now accepted by the directors. “Because I was holding senior colleagues to account on all decisions, they began accepting my recommendations for building the business or adjusting procedures more readily.”

Through the deeper, more trusted relationships she has built, Shanthy is seeing a stronger team ethic at the Belsize Park operation. “Before, people knew some board members and managers took different approaches to procedures, so staff always felt they were taking sides," Shanthy explains. "We've got past that feeling, which is better for the business and our customers."

Shanthy is now accepted as having board-level responsibility and is helping lead the store's development. She says her more confident communication and greater focus has had a ripple-through effect in the business. "After 100 days, I have a clearer idea of what needs to be done and what should be said and how. I have more time to help and encourage my colleagues. They now say I'm a bean-counter with a great personality," she laughs.

Reflection

In this step, you will have seen why the skills you need as a leader will be different to the ones you have needed in the past. You will understand that being a leader has different skill requirements to those in your team; and whilst you need to understand and demonstrate some empathy with the team members and their skills, the leader's skill set is different.

The following process will allow you to have a better understanding of the skills required in your role and how satisfied you are with the required skills. In addition, you will create a plan to learn these skills and set up an accountability process to ensure that you achieve your goals.

In the following Step 5: Communicating with clarity – you will also learn one more skill about how to communicate with clarity, and this will build a better relationship with yourself.

Improving Your Skill Set – Exercise

The worksheets in the following pages are examples, but you can download the full size, full colour, ready to print worksheets from ZeroToAuthenticHero.com and follow these instructions:

Part 1: Take the worksheet for this step (worksheet 1) and then spend a few minutes sitting in silence; try to step outside of your current role and into the shoes of a neutral observer. Use the job description of human resource manager, and your own knowledge of the role. List the top eight skills on the worksheet, with one in each of the segments.

Part 2: Change roles back to yourself again. Now, deeply and authentically, consider how satisfied you are with your ability in each of these skills. Score each of the skills, using this technique:

Score each skill as a percentage (out of 100) and use increments of 10 (0, 10, 20, 30 ... etc.), but only use each once. This is done intentionally to really make you rank your skills, as opposed to just placing an average or mid-ranking score against each.

During this process, make sure you treat yourself in alignment with your values, and with equal dignity—there is no need to inflate your ego if you score well, but also there is no need to become frustrated where there is a lower score.

Part 3: Now that you have ranked your satisfaction with the skills required for the role, select those where you need to make improvements; it's good to focus on a small number at first, which is realistic and achievable.

List these on the plan (worksheet 2), setting out your skills goal at the top, and current situation at the bottom. Then, work through the steps you are going to take (and when you are going to take them) to reach your skills goal. Take the first steps on your plan and create a timeline for completion.

Part 4: Create an accountability process. This is a way for you to ask for help from another person and check in with them on a regular basis. Using clear communication, ask for their support and a structured approach, without excuse or blame; this is an incredibly powerful process to help keep you on track.

IMPROVING YOUR SKILL SET (1)

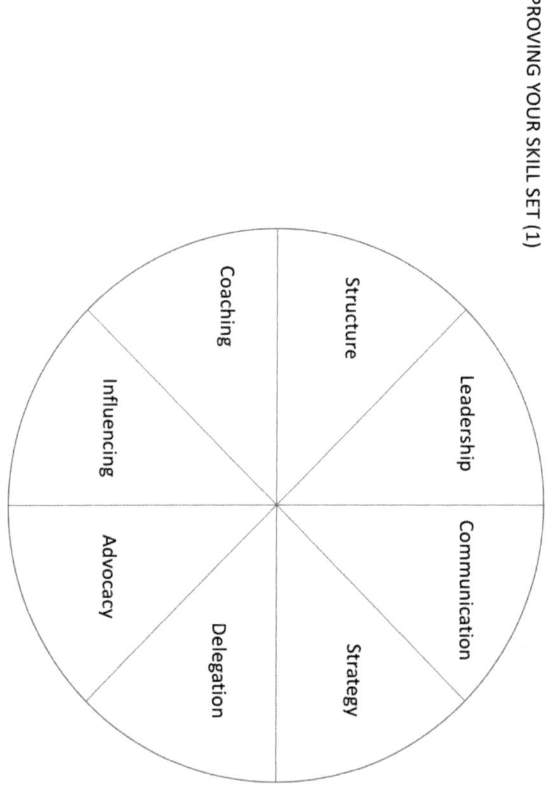

IMPROVING YOUR SKILL SET (2)

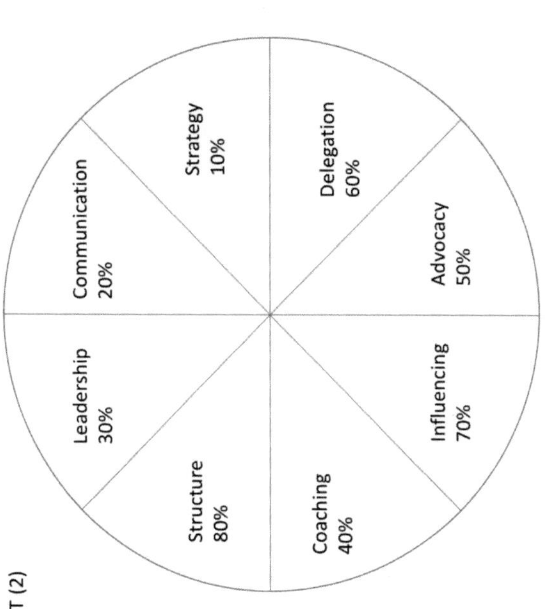

IMPROVING YOUR SKILL SET - PLAN

Goal Mthly	Leadership Be seen to be a good leader	Strategy Develop a clear 3 year plan	Communication Have good communication with everyone
4	Create an authentic approach	Work with Daniel and Julie to create clear 3 year strategy	Ensure program needs are being delivered
3	Leave behind what is no longer authentic to myself	Create broad strategy plan	Test different options – directive, influencing, supportive
2	Understand impact of these on self and others	Complete online strategy tutorials	Work through communication options for each person
1	Look at my leadership heros	Read the blue ocean strategy book that was recommended.	Observe how each individual communicates
Start	Dominant style – how does that become authentic	What strategy approach do I take	How do I communicate best with very different people

Accountability Process: Fortnightly check in with Daniel Frohwein

Notes

Step 5: Communicating with Clarity

"Justification is the lie you use to pretend that you are not in charge."
Raymond Aaron – *New York Times* Top 10 Bestselling Author

In this step, you will find out how important it is to have clean and clear communication, but also why it helps everyone else when you tell them what you want. You will learn about the difference between YOU and I, language, and communicating through the values. This will create a better relationship with yourself, and will achieve more with less stress.

You will have your own beliefs; and when you bring greater awareness to these, you can understand why you communicate in the way you do, and then you can choose to change your communication style to have a much more positive effect. Further, the really challenging time to do this is when you are in conflict either with yourself or another.

Clarity is Much Sought

I asked leaders to gift their wisdom to support a growing community of purpose-led leaders. The key findings show a growing need for investment in time, removal of personal blockages, greater clarity, and developing authenticity.

I was surprised that more than eight out of every ten leaders were seeking more clarity and courage in their leadership roles. Edward Woyakovsky, an entrepreneur specialising in hotel groups, says that a "much improved clarity in the business is required by many leaders, and this can support a better reputation both within the company and to the outside world."

When it comes to clarity for leaders, the most critical issues, we have been told, are around purpose, strategy, and vision. Second to these are values, which appear in many businesses but remain poorly communicated and, therefore, unclear. The key message here is that clarity needs to be communicated, but this needs to start with the leader having clarity themselves.

Who Smashed the Well?

In the early 2000s, a coalition of troops from many countries invaded Afghanistan in the hunt for Taliban insurgents. This is not a story about the war or any political or moral debate but simply a story of one true event that took place during that time. One British Army regiment had a week of rest and rehabilitation near a small village some miles away from the front line. They noticed that the women of the village had to walk for many miles each day to fetch drinking water and to wash the family's clothes in the river.

The Army decided that they would utilise their rest time, skills, and resources to build a well for the village. This would provide fresh water in the village for drinking and washing, therefore improving the women's lives and preventing them from having to walk the long distance to the river each day.

So, on the first day, the men and women of the British Army toiled long and hard to dig a well very deep into the dry ground of the village until they reached the water table; quickly, the well filled with fresh drinkable water. The soldiers then built a stone wall around the top and added a wooden winding mechanism to lower buckets and raise fresh water from the ground.

The following day, the second day, the soldiers returned to the village to find that the winding mechanism has been smashed and thrown into the well, and all the stones around the wall at the top had also been pushed into the deep hole. However, the soldiers felt it was their duty to help the village and to build bridges with the community; therefore, they rebuilt the well. In addition, the soldiers built a fence around the well, which they locked at night in order to protect it from being destroyed again.

On the third day, the soldiers again returned to find that the fence, winding mechanism, and the wall had been smashed and thrown down into the well. Again, the soldiers believed that they were doing what was required by building a well; they set about removing the stones from the hole and rebuilding the wall and a new mechanism. This time, not only was the fence rebuilt, but a TV camera was added so that the soldiers could observe any activity at night around the well.

The morning of the fourth day came, and the soldiers arrived at the village to find that the camera, the fence, the winding mechanism, and wall, all again, were at the bottom of the well; but, of course, they had video recording of what had taken place overnight.

The question was: who had smashed the well?

Most of the soldiers believed that it was the men of the village who had destroyed the well, because the soldiers were imposing something new upon the village, which the elders had not agreed to have built. Some of the soldiers believed it was the young boys in the village, who had nothing better to do and were simply causing mischief. A few of the soldiers believed that Taliban insurgents were travelling to the village, across several miles of country each night, just to frustrate the Army's work.

Who do you think was destroying the well?

When the video evidence was reviewed, the soldiers were startled to see that it was actually the women of the village who were destroying the well. These were the actual women that the soldiers thought they were helping by saving them from having to walk several miles and carry large pots of water back to the village each day. However, when they spoke to the women at the village, the soldiers found out that the women's walk to the river to wash the clothes and collect the water was actually the only time that the men allowed the women to leave the village, and this is their time to socialise together and play with their children, whilst avoiding being in servitude to their husbands.

The soldiers believed that they were helping the village, but at no time during the process had they communicated with clarity what they had planned—they would have found that the well would not be welcome. They believed they knew the need but had not asked what was wanted, or indeed listened to what was needed.

You and I Language

I need to share with you how often people say to me, "Well, you know," or "You would love this restaurant." This is very kind, and always said with best intentions, but it's also a good example of *you language* as opposed to *I language*. Guess what: I don't know what's going on in your head, and I have absolutely no idea what beliefs you have that are driving those words. You don't know what's in my head or what my beliefs are. So, I choose not to assume that I know what some other person's beliefs are.

This is the difference between *you* and *I* language. Speaking to another person, and referring to them all of the time as *you*, is imposing your beliefs, thoughts, and judgements onto the other. What right do you have to do this? In my opinion, none.

Take personal responsibility for your language and speak about *I*. In order to do this, however, you need a deep understanding of your own beliefs and how they are contributing to communication. Taking responsibility does not infer fault or blame. It's just taking responsibility. By all means, say to the other person: "I enjoy that restaurant, and you may like it too," which states your position and leaves the other with a choice.

So, speak for yourself, and don't make judgements or assumptions about others. In writing this book, I acknowledge that some parts may feel like instructions, but I—in this case, you— have a choice whether you buy and read the book, or otherwise. That's entirely your choice; but I have tried to avoid teaching through the steps, and I prefer to show what others have done and leave you to use the exercise at the end of each step to find out for yourself.

Taking personal responsibility also extends to blame. What happens when you are late for a meeting? When the head of the meeting welcomes you into a room full of other people who arrived on time and have already covered the first few points of the agenda, what do you say? Do you take responsibility, or blame the traffic, the trains, an accident, or somebody else?

Instead of just blaming something or someone else, ask yourself, "What did I prioritise over being on time?" Did you stay in bed that extra 10 minutes or stop for a coffee on the way? Truly, why am I late? Then, if you have truly found the authentic reason, choose whether you need to apologise: "Sorry, I slept in." Or, use gratitude to the leader of the meeting for allowing you to join in: "Thank you for allowing me to join late."

When do you actually say, "It was my fault; I didn't leave enough time for the journey?" You are no longer using justification or blame of others—justification is the lie you use to pretend that you are not in charge.

Communicating Through the Values

Having worked out your own values earlier in this process, consider how you communicate with yourself in alignment with them. Select your first value and think through whether your style and delivery of the internal chat inside your head is aligned with this, or otherwise. How should you change your thoughts or words to yourself to be more aligned? Consider this for all of your chosen values.

How do you communicate with yourself through your values?

I talked about self-limiting beliefs earlier, and you may have been repeating these to yourself over the years. You will be aware of some of these beliefs, and some others will be buried deep in your subconscious. Only by bringing awareness to your thoughts and feelings, and then being curious as to where these are coming from, can you learn more about them. Consider this for all of your chosen values.

There is a four-step process to work through this, which is explained in the exercise on the following pages. This simple, four-step process can be used in all communication with yourself.

It Starts Within

A Yorkshire GP surgery's practice manager experienced misunderstandings over roles and responsibilities after a reorganisation. A one-on-one coaching day for the team with

Mandala Leaders, requested by the practice's managing partner, has resolved these issues by helping them better understand priorities, ways of working, and how they could better collaborate in a stressful workplace. With a clearer view of their objectives and how to reach them, the practice manager is driving the surgery's new business plan. Mandala Leaders' coaching session was surprising her because it guided her to her own realisation of what needed to change: the answer was that she needed to change their own approach to communication.

Problem

As GP surgeries across Britain are pushed to their limits meeting care demands from an ageing population, Practice One in Bridlington—a Yorkshire seaside resort with the third oldest age profile of any community in Britain—has dug deeper than most to reinforce its crucial team ethic.

Key practice managers' roles and duties became confused after the surgery was reorganised. Practice One managing partner, Tom Milligan, saw that running a 6,000-patient surgery prevented fresh thinking or finding ways for colleagues to play to each other's strengths. He asked Mandala Leaders, a consultancy dedicated to transforming the life of an organisation and the communities it serves, to provide one-on-one coaching, to improve the manager's understanding and refocus the way they went about their work.

Practice manager, Jan Peacock, responsible for practice's administration of NHS funding and reimbursement, and her deputy, who was focusing on staff administration as well as practice funding and incentives, were finding overlaps in their duties. There were also increasing misunderstandings over how best to run the surgery's busy front office.

Managing partner, Tom Milligan, set Mandala Leaders three tough targets for the coaching day: restore trust, clarify the support needed for her role and responsibilities, and enlist Jan in preparing an outline business plan for the practice. "If we could get a clear approach to the plan, I knew we would solve things," explains Tom Milligan.

Solution

The Mandala team organised a single day coaching session, focused entirely on the practice manager and their needs. Dispensing with classroom-style teaching, Mandala consultants Nick Bradley and Daniel Frohwein began with a series of exercises to build greater trust, and they followed with sessions that explored the individual's approach to others, their methods, and how they ran the practice.

Despite being a recipient of training throughout her career, this time, Jan Peacock found herself being challenged rather than taught. It was about Jan's personal journey and how this impacted on others. "I'd never been on a course like it. The emphasis was on what I thought my role was and why or how I came to be where I was. Nick and Daniel didn't tell me things; they guided me to my own conclusions."

Benefits

Jan returned to Bridlington after Mandala coaching, with a far better appreciation of her team's roles, approach, and skills, and how to drive the practice's commercial plans. The practice management team now work more closely; colleagues have noticed greater harmony in staff meetings, rotas, and dealing with patients and suppliers.

The coaching has added wider, longer-term value for Practice One. “I focus better on priorities rather than simply trying to get through emails and calls,” says Jan Peacock. “I’ve found a way to step back and communicate more effectively.”

The improved team work has delivered a focused and happier workplace, with Practice One playing a key part of the NHS East Riding of Yorkshire Clinical Commissioning Group, winning the well-known Health Service Journal Awards 2016 for its contribution to closer working between GP groups and local council on public health.

Tom Milligan appreciates the rapid way that acceptance of change was instilled in his practice by Mandala’s consultants: “As a GP, my whole business is about behavioural change. For any attendees to grasp the need for change, they’ve got to feel equal with the course leader and themselves. Mandala Leaders’ coaching clearly rebuilt trust and empathy with Jan and gave her a real opportunity to sort things out and release her true potential.”

Reflection

You have found that there is a need for clear and concise communication with yourself, without judgement or blame. Indeed, sharing gratitude is an incredibly powerful thing to bring better connections with yourself too. This is just the start of your journey into better communication—starting with yourself.

Use the worksheets and the exercise on the following pages to work through the detail of this, and create an accountability process whilst you grow deeper into awareness of the way in which you speak to yourself. Try and practice this for a couple of weeks before moving onto the next step so that you can really make it part of your daily life.

In the following Step 6: Living Your Legacy – you will start to think about not only what legacy you can leave, but actually how you can live with your legacy. How do you start to create this and deliver this for the people around you now? How do you live with it now?

Communicating with Clarity – Exercise

The worksheets in the following pages are examples, but you can download the full size, full colour, ready to print worksheets from ZeroToAuthenticHero.com and follow these instructions:

Part 1: Use worksheet 1, and follow these four steps to this process. There is space on the worksheet to record and consider four communication scenarios, or use four of your values; duplicate the worksheet for more scenarios/values.

a. Self-Judgements: This is just like when you make judgments of others; you also often make judgments of yourself. You have critical concepts about your knowledge, looks, and ability, and these are often driven by feelings of shame, fear, or guilt. These judgements often play out in a desperate needs to attain something like money, beauty, or connection, and sometimes to avoid or run away from conflict, fear, and shame.
   Consider how these self-judgements may affect how you communicate with yourself.

b. Self-empathy: This is where you become more aware through curiosity of your own feelings, and identify which needs may be missing. Think about all of your basic needs. You need to take a quiet moment to recognize the self-judgement, and enquire what is driving that—what is lying behind the judgement? In order to gain awareness of your beliefs, ask yourself: “I choose to [action] because I want [need].” And then you can make a conscious decision whether you wish to remain in this state or leave that historic belief behind.
   Think about how this self-empathy may help you understand yourself better.

c. Expressing anger: Use the value of personal responsibility to really take accountability of what you have done yourself to create anger in yourself (like when you are angry because you are late for a meeting), which may drive feelings of shame —and it's just because you slept in late.
When have you been angry, and did you consider your responsibility in creating that feeling first?

d. Expressing gratitude: Everyone yearns to be genuinely appreciated, but do not assume that other people know the intensity of your appreciation. Again, gratitude is a judgement, but this time it's a positive one. It is still a judgement. Statements, like "You are a good person," are just judgments that have no foundation, and can sometimes be taken by other listeners as, "So, why don't they think I'm a good person too?"
Consider how you express gratitude; be specific in what you are thankful for, and avoid making judgements.

Part 2: Create an accountability process. This is a way for you to ask for help from another person and check in with them on a regular basis. Using clear communication, ask for their support and a structured approach, without excuse or blame; this is an incredibly powerful process to help keep you on track.

COMMUNICATING WITH CLARITY - SELF

	Situation 1 **Equal dignity**	Situation 2 **Personal responsibility**	Situation 3 **Personal integrity**	Situation 4 **Authenticity**
Self Judgement	I work so hard that I am really tired at the end of the day	I am angry because I was late for a meeting	I didn't tell my friend that I didn't want to meet as I'm too busy	I feel obliged to go to my brother's birthday party even though I don't want to
Self Empathy	I choose to chase money and don't take care of myself	I chose to stay at home longer to finish breakfast	In reality I am scared that I may upset them	In reality I don't mind going as it's their special time
Expressing Anger	I'm angry that I have to do everything myself	I'm really upset with myself for lying in bed when I should have been eating breakfast	I'm angry that I can't be honest with my friend that they are draining me with their negative stuff	I'm angry about how my brother treats me and I don't respect him
Expressing Gratitude	I am grateful for the money I make	I have gratitude for sharing breakfast	I am grateful to have this friend but I need to express my needs	I can choose to go and enjoy the event if I leave the past behind
Result	I now choose to delegate more non-money making tasks and pay others to deliver these.	I enjoy breakfast and I get up when the alarm goes off – and I make it to the meeting in time.	I tell my friend that I need to look after my needs and not theirs	I go to the party, stay for an hour and come home happy

Accountability Process: Weekly review with Julie Clements

Notes

Notes

Step 6: Living Your Legacy

"I'm not interested in my legacy.
I made up a word: live-acy.
I'm more interested in living."
John Glenn, the first American astronaut to orbit the Earth.

A legacy is often thought of as being a sum of money you can leave to the next generation. Maybe it's the family home, investments, or cash. But a financial legacy is only one type of resource you can leave behind. You can also leave skills, knowledge, a support network, or a structure that can help others to develop and continue to grow whatever you leave.

This also doesn't have to be a legacy gifted to others at the end of your life; think of legacy as a way to consider what you will leave in, say, five years' time, and start working towards that now. Those people who have a five-year plan tend to achieve more and become more successful, personally and professionally.

Think what you could achieve if you had a plan for every five years for the rest of your life. Do you want to leave a legacy, or deliver that whilst you are still alive? Do you want to live your legacy?

But it's also not about leaving this behind for others after a defined period of time. It's about creating something, enjoying it for the duration, living with it, and then letting others have the benefit of what you leave.

In this step, you will learn how to create and live your legacy, and how to ensure that you deliver this for the benefit of yourself, which others will also benefit from later.

Legacy Needs Greater Promotion

I asked leaders to gift their wisdom to support a growing community of purpose-led leaders. The key findings show a growing need for investment in time, removal of personal blockages, greater clarity, and developing authenticity.

Only half of the leaders said they had time to develop a greater legacy and reputation. They told me that there is often too much focus on the day-to-day issues, which reduces the opportunity to look to the future.

"Create a legacy that other people adopt," says financial services veteran, Steve Barningham, as this ensures the team is on the same page and working to the same goals as the business leader.

Where Do You Plant the Tree?

Where do you think it's best to plant a young tree: a clearing in an old-growth forest or an open field?

Ecologists tell us that a young tree grows better when it's planted in an area with older trees. The reason, it seems, is that the roots of the young tree are able to follow the pathways created by older trees, and implant themselves more deeply.

Over time, the roots of many trees may actually graft themselves to one another, creating an intricate, interdependent foundation hidden under the ground.

In this way, stronger trees share resources with weaker ones so that the whole forest becomes healthier. That's legacy: an interconnection across time, with a need for those who have come before us, and a responsibility to those who come after us.

You Can Enjoy Your Legacy

There is an exercise often used that will help in projecting your thinking forward. It centres on a death-bed scene and your last wishes: the last words of wisdom you might imagine you would wish to impart. You are asked to imagine what you are leaving behind to the next generation.

But the truth is, you don't need to imagine that you are about to depart this plane to decide what you wish to leave behind. Words of wisdom and ideas are resources; and whilst you may leave knowledge, you may also leave property, skills, structure, processes, and customers.

You can leave behind a legacy when you leave the job where you are currently employed. You can be thinking of what legacy you wish to leave behind after the next job you are about to start. You can choose a set timeframe—say, 5 years from now—what will you have left behind at that time?

But you can actually live this legacy both whilst you build it and enjoy it—is that a new concept to you about legacy?

So, in the following pages, is a slightly different process to follow. This will result in you taking the first steps to have greater clarity on your legacy—which is for you to enjoy—and how you are going to create this. You will end up with a small number of things that you can live with and enjoy, then share with others, and then leave for the next generation.

I Created My Legacy

A recruitment specialist, focused on the banking sector, moved back to the UK after working in Singapore for many years; he wanted to create a business that supported his family, to include a new house and school fees for his daughter. Working with the one-day, *Living Your Legacy* process, by Mandala Leaders, they created clear goals of what they wanted to achieve in 5 years, and what the benefit would be for his wife and daughter, both in the medium and long term, and he based his business model around achieving these goals.

Mandala Leaders' coaching session was an awakening for the individual as they realised that by building his business in a certain way, he could more easily achieve all of his family goals, rather than simply running hard just to pay the bills each month. This gave him a far greater incentive to achieve his full potential, both personally and professionally.

Problem

Having moved back to the UK so that his daughter could attend school, Nigel Close had left a large successful financial service recruitment company and chosen to go out alone for the first time. This meant building contacts, both in banks and with bankers who wanted a new job, and trying to find the balance between throwing the net very wide or focusing on certain roles and geographies.

Initially, Nigel had "thrown his effort into everything that moved, hoping that something would stick" so to speak, but this was exhausting and unproductive. He was not able to make all the meetings he had planned, didn't have time to properly follow up, and was not providing the best possible service that he wanted to supply.

Nigel had a need to focus, to play to his strengths, and to decide if a solo business was appropriate or whether he could grow this through a partnership or an acquisition approach. There was much to consider, so Nigel asked for help from Nick Bradley of Mandala Leaders.

Solution

The Mandala team organised a half day coaching session, focusing on helping Nigel to gain clarity on what he wanted to achieve for himself and his family in the next 5 years—what the legacy was that he wanted to create and then live with.

Nigel reflected that he wanted a family home without a mortgage, and to be able to pay for school fees for a private education for his daughter. With some support, Nigel then worked through a personal financial model to work out what he needed to earn in order to pay off a mortgage and school fees, so that in this period of time, his legacy could be created.

In order to achieve this financial model, Nick and Nigel then looked at different business structures and the risks of these, as well as the different areas of business roles to focus on, and chose key geographic locations. This was to be the core business for at least the first year, but it was also able to adjust and adapt as time progressed. Nigel chose an individual approach but also posted available jobs on larger listing websites in order to achieve a wider audience.

In addition, he chose to focus on Manchester (where he lived) and London geographically, as these were the larger markets, and he chose only ten possible clients and focused on mid-tier banking professional roles. This gave Nigel a clearly defined market, allowed him to understand the demands of this space quickly, and build a presence and expertise in just a few months.

Further, we agreed that Nigel should focus on where he adds value, and he has, therefore, chosen to outsource back-office needs, such as finance and technology.

Benefits

One year into the process, and Nigel has managed to create a good set of clients, happy candidates, and regular repeat business from his clients. He is working more in Manchester, with just occasional trips into London, so his work/life balance is also improved. Nigel had adopted a strategy of meeting every candidate he puts forward for a role, to ensure quality and consistency, but has flexed this by reducing the short lists from 6 to 4, and using video conferencing when necessary.

He has started to pay off the mortgage on his family home, and his daughter is happy having completed her first few terms at a new private school. He is confident that this approach will not only create a legacy in 5 years of having a successful business, which could afford to pay Nigel sufficiently to achieve his personal goals, but his daughter would be receiving a fine education, and he and his wife would be mortgage and stress free. An additional and even unintended legacy was that in the longer term, the mortgage-free house could be used to help his daughter get onto the housing ladder herself.

Reflection

The legacy step in this program is usually the most emotional part of the journey; so, if you have already felt a whole range of emotions, then I ask you to find the courage to continue, as this will help you to create a better life for yourself and those that you care about. Work through the tears and the anger by understating your beliefs connected to them, and create a legacy of which you are proud.

Use the worksheets and the exercise on the following pages to work through the details of this step, and create a legacy plan whilst you grow deeper into awareness of yourself. Try and kick off your action plan for a couple of weeks before moving onto the next step, so that you can really make it part of your daily life.

In the following Step 7: Building in resilience – you will learn how to build in resilience to help you to face the daily challenges and emotional battles that you always experience, and create a plan to improve your soul, and your physical, mental, and social emotions.

Living Your Legacy – Exercise

Here is a new process to follow, which will result in you having greater clarity on your legacy that you wish to live, and how you are going to create this. You will end up with a small number of goals to achieve, which you can live, share with others, and leave in due course.

The worksheets in the following pages are examples, but you can download the full size, full colour, ready to print worksheets from ZeroToAuthenticHero.com and follow these instructions:

Part 1: This can be completed on Worksheet (1).

Write down or record the story of your life: the meaningful parts rather than the indulgences and pleasures you may have had. What have you done that you are proud of (at work, at home, as part of whatever community you are a member)?

Pick your top five achievements and then identify any patterns or insights—what does this tell you about yourself? If you thought you knew what advice or wisdom you might wish to share, think again! Then, go deeper. What else? What above the rest stands out as the most important value, or action, or thought?

Part 2: This can be completed on Worksheet (2).

Take a moment to slow down whatever you're doing; allow your breathing to settle down and, if already relaxed, take a few slow deep breaths. You are about to answer one of the most important questions of your life. Take your time. Take as long as you need (around fifteen minutes is a guide).

Think about these questions:
What reputation do you want to live with?
What resources could you enjoy and share with others?
What values could you live by and share?
What is the advice or wisdom you most want to remind yourself of and share with others?

Part 3: This can be completed on Worksheet (3).

This is the opportunity to find out what legacy you want to live. Take a few moments to consider what you chose:

Is it to be happy?
To be true to yourself?
To be kind to yourself/to others/to the planet/to all three?
Follow your dreams?
Take care of your family?
Leave behind assets or money?
Hope that people write and say good things about you?

It's funny how often many people made some of their biggest life choices around making money or around another form of ego-expression, rather than realising their potential for greatness. What else did you wish to live and leave as your legacy, and why was that? You may wish others to have the same as you have had. You may wish for them to have more of different resources and advice.

But also consider what you want for yourself in this time-frame—we are talking about 5 years—what do you want and where do you want to be? What legacy do you want to live—do you want family, a new house, a new job?

Part 4: This can be completed on Worksheet (4).

This is the final stage, and you are going to build out a simple plan to give clear goals and a direction of travel to achieve this legacy that you can live.

a. Complete the worksheet, with a short summary of each goal you need to achieve to live your legacy, in each column across the top line.

b. Then, in the second row, summarise who is going to enjoy this legacy. Is it your children, family, work place, or customers? Or, indeed, a much wider community? Indeed, are you going to benefit too? How do you benefit from this legacy?

c. Then, at the bottom line of each column, reflect where you are today in relation to that legacy goal.

d. Then, work out what 3 or 4 steps you need to take to deliver that legacy. This period of creation of your legacy should be where you live it—enjoy it, and benefit from it too.

e. Finally, develop more clarity on the first step: when are you going to do this; what resources do you need; who can you ask for help; what is the very first thing you are going to do, and when are you going to do that?

This is your legacy plan. Make sure you follow this and drive each and every step.

Only by doing this will you be able to look back—when you leave this job, in 5 years' time, or even on your deathbed—and be able to authentically say, "I lived this." Have a clear vision of the destination, as well as the way you get there. Be humble and courageous towards whatever meets you on the way. Stay aware of the signposts and signals in the distance, and indeed those around you at each step on the road.

Part 5: Finally, create an accountability process. This is a way for you to ask for help from another person and check in with them on a regular basis. Using clear communication, ask for their support and a structured approach, without excuse or blame; this is an incredibly powerful process to help keep you on track.

LIVING YOUR LEGACY (1)

What is the story of your life? I have moved form country to country working for large recruitment companies and building a new business for them in each territory. I have worked hard in building out new businesses and creating networks I work hard and have no time for my family I travel too much
What are your top 5 achievements? 1. All of the businesses have grown well 2. I have a great wife and beautiful daughter 3. I have enough money in the bank for 50% of the dream home 4. I am well regarded in the global market (but not UK) 5. I have started a successful business before
What is the most important value or action or thought? I am able to grow a business form scratch I am good at networking I want a good work/life balance

LIVING YOUR LEGACY (2)

What reputation do you want to have? Professional and dependable – delivering good service and great candidates to clients A family man who is part of the local community
What resources could you share with others? Property and money Time Knowledge of building a business
What values could you share? Professionalism Creativity Drive
What is the advice or wisdom you most want to share? Take action and the results will be achieved

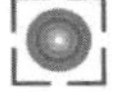

LIVING YOUR LEGACY (3)

What is your legacy that your want to live?

I want to have a house without mortgage
I want to have a daughter in private education
Work/Life balance to improve therefore more time with family.

Support the wider community of recruiters
Leave a sustainable well regarded business

LIVING YOUR LEGACY – PLAN

Goal	Business to be successful	Contribute to the community	Work / Life balance	
4	Measure turnover, cash flow and value	Leverage my work with others to obtain greater benefit – it's not about just my contribution	Ensure that I meet a friend at least once per week (evening pub or Sunday lunch with family)	
3	Outsource back office work functions	Commit to do this 0.5 days per week for the next 12 months – set clear goals to achieve	Outsource back office work functions	
2	Drive business in a focused way	Network there and find how best I can use my skills and experience to the community advantage	Find a community interest	
1	Build business plan and goals	Identify and join a wider community group	Commit to school events, plays, parents evening, sports day etc.	
Start	Initial business ideas	Nothing at present	Fully committed at work	

Accountability Process: Check in with my coach fortnightly

Notes

Notes

Step 7: Building in Resilience

"Obviously, resilience matters. I was no stranger to adversity, but it's different when it's personal."
David Petraeus – Commander, U.S. Forces Afghanistan

There are many challenges in life, and sometimes they all feel like they have come at the same time. Some days you may feel you have the burden of the world on your shoulders, and some days you have an easy-going time—just for 3 things to go wrong at once!!

In addition, the ever-increasing pace of change in the world, led through improved transportation links, quicker technology and growing demand for rolling information through cable news channels and social media is leading to growing demands on your time. These lead to stresses; waiting until these hit and start to have damaging effects on your emotional and physical wellbeing is one approach, but building stronger resilience and working to avoid the stress is a preferred approach.

I find it is best to actually carve out some time each day for yourself. I know this may sound selfish, but just like the aircraft safety briefing where you are told to put on your oxygen mask before you help others, it is best to make sure that you are in your best place so that you can help others more effectively.

What does he mean? Well, this is when you are practicing your new behaviours and delivering your plans—you should take some time out to check on how you are practicing those new habits, and that you are actually practicing them well. You can also reflect on how you can perhaps practice them better.

It's also about having balance between working hard and relaxing, friends and family, diet and exercise, and creating some head space in order to have time and space to reflect and learn how you are doing.

So, if you are running around all of the time, you will become exhausted and stressed quickly, but if you practice a daily program of actions for yourself, you will have a less stressful approach to the challenges that will come; and you will be able to tackle these more effectively and easily.

This is a powerful way to build resilience.

Why Did You Have to Burn?

The word, *resilience,* is now used everywhere, often in ways that drain it of meaning and link it to vague concepts like *character.* But resilience doesn't have to be an empty or vague concept. In fact, decades of research have revealed a lot about how it works. This research shows that resilience is, ultimately, a set of skills that can be taught.

There are many versions of the story of the phoenix rising from the ashes. There are many different ways in which the bird reached its death; but in each, it rises the same way: out of its own ashes and into the sun. This myth of the phoenix, that symbol of endurance, began in Arabian and Egyptian folklore, and was brought to the West by Herodotus, 2,500 years ago.

We have an ancient attraction to stories of resilience, but recently, the word itself has joined popular culture. Deriving from the Latin form, *to jump again*, resilience has sprung into new life as a catchword in international development and Silicon Valley, and among parenting pundits. Numerous people speak on the topic, with most focussing on toughening up your investment portfolio, or your toddler. It's a word that is somehow so conveniently vacant that it manages to be both profound and profoundly hollow.

The word has also started swallowing up previous jargon, like survival of the fittest, supplanting, and sustainability. At a United Nations event, the General Secretary, Ban Ki-moon, described resilience by saying that "we cannot stop disasters, but we can anticipate the risks and reduce them."

But the question that I really like to ask is, "Why rise from the ashes without asking why you had to burn?"

<u>The Four Gateways</u>

The way to build resilience is represented by the four gateways on the *Zero to Authentic Hero* logo. These gateways each represent a channel for you to connect with others, information, exercise, diet, etc., which are outside of your own self.

They are all ways to nourish yourself, both physically and emotionally; and, when maintained in balance, they can help to build stronger resilience.

The four gateways are:

Soul

I want to be really careful about what this means. Some people prefer the term spiritual, but some do not. I always believed this to be a religious phrase connected with your God. However, it does, of course, mean different things to different people. For me, it's whatever that means to you. And that's good. For me, personally, it is a higher power, or better described as a higher purpose. It can also be described a little differently—what nourishes your soul?

For you, it can mean whatever it means to you. For me, the question is, why am I here? What is my purpose? Why am I on this planet? What is my purpose in life? What am I here to do? That is the soul connection for me. However, what it means to somebody else is just what to means to them. There is no need for there to be any judgement about what they believe.

In order to keep connected to your soul power, you can use prayer, meditation, silence, etc. Maybe you have a deep connection with your religious power and have a regular prayer practice. Maybe just a simple breathing meditation. Use whatever is good for you, every day, to reconnect with your higher purpose, and make sure that you continue to travel in the right direction.

If you don't have a method to practice this connection to your soul, then I usually recommend an app on your phone, which can lead you through a simple breathing process where you can check in with your soul and ensure you remain aligned.

Physical

This is being able to do all the physical things you need to do. It's exercising to the best of your ability, and to run and be active and do all the things you need to do in your life. It is also eating in the way that's right for you. It is exercising in the appropriate way and eating in the appropriate way.

What is your exercise regime, and how consistently do you exercise? Do you play sports, go to the gym, swim, run, practice yoga, or some other exercise? Do you walk up the stairs instead of taking the escalator or elevator? How do you exercise, and how consistently do you practice?

How is your diet and drug and alcohol consumption? What are your food choices, and how consistently do you practice these? Have you managed to reduce your drug or alcohol intake, and keep it down? What is your balance of meat, fish, carbohydrates, and fruit and vegetables? What is the appropriate drug and alcohol intake that you want for yourself?

Mental

This is stimulating the mental faculties; when we are learning, we grow the grey cells. So, instead of watching TV, read a book. Consider a book that is aligned to your purpose. If your purpose is teaching children about maths, then read a book about teaching children about maths.

Listen to podcasts, watch appropriate videos, go to conferences, and learn from others where you can support your purpose. This isn't just a personal crusade, however, as you can also engage in discussion and debate with others who follow a similar path, and learn from them.

Social

The social dimension is included under a belief that the emotional life is also supported from an interaction with others. If you are living on your own in a cave, you will feel a very different emotional experience than if you were out socializing, networking, and connecting with other people.

If you practice the habit of connecting with other people, you are building those relationships, and if you practice the habit of clear communication, you can build very deep and meaningful friendships that support your emotional wellbeing.

Some people may have a more extroverted personality, where they draw energy from others; some may have a more introverted personality, and they draw their energy from their time spent alone.

So, the balance of personal time and social time will differ for everyone, but the key point here is that you do not have to take a journey alone—you can always ask for help.

Balance Brings Presence

Higher Education planning manager, Helen Sharp, has refocused her soul, physical, mental, and social plans, using the *Zero to Authentic Hero* resilience process. The key benefit is a better balance, and allowing herself to prioritise herself, at times, when juggling work and family commitments. The accountability process has driven new behaviours, which are rapidly bringing action, as opposed to just the idea of action.

Situation

With busy work pressure and a number of challenges being passed to her from many different directions, Helen was feeling stretched; and whilst she was a regular fitness fan, she felt out of alignment with the other areas that nourished her soul. Her growing work responsibilities, overlaid with studying for a master's qualification, needed to be balanced with family commitments and time out for herself.

Solution

Helen turned to the *Zero To Authentic Hero* program, from Mandala Leaders, a consultancy dedicated to transforming the life of individuals and the communities they serve, for assistance. Mandala Leaders' founder, Nick Bradley, devised a resilience program for her.

In one session, Helen worked through the areas of soul, physical, mental, and social, and made a plan for each area, which was achievable, balanced, and timely. Whilst not wanting to undertake four or five actions in each area simultaneously, Helen has created a program that builds up over the first six weeks and can be reviewed and revised at each stage.

Through this program, Helen identified that, whilst she had been working hard in the gym, her balance with mental and cultural learning was not aligned; she, therefore, chose to make a commitment to a weekly event, which fulfilled this need. In addition, she has enjoyed reading sector-focused publications in support of her master's work, and now wants to continue reading these, once qualified.

Benefits

Helen is now feeling in better alignment, is enjoying her work more, and is feeling the benefits, both for herself and family, as the personal work is quickly reflected with others. "Whilst it may seem simple, I needed reminding that time for myself has wider benefits, and I am now more energetic, focused in my work, and able to be fully present for my family."

Reflection

You have found that resilience comes with balance and a desire to avoid the challenges in the first place. Living in alignment, with a clear purpose and a set of values, does help to significantly reduce the emotional knocks that you receive on a daily basis, and working through all of the other steps in this process will support you too.

There is need for a plan to become resilient—it doesn't just happen overnight—and you should build this up slowly over the next few weeks. In addition, it is imperative that you include an accountability plan to share your progress with others and ask them to challenge you to keep on track—or, indeed, join you on the journey!!

Use the worksheets and the exercise on the following pages to work through the details of this program, and create a resilience plan whilst you grow deeper into awareness of the way in which you manage your soul, mental, physical, and social emotions. Try and practice this for a couple of weeks before moving onto the next step, so that you can really make it part of your daily life.

In the final chapter, *The 100-Day Plan*, you will find a process to help you to bring together all of your learning and action plans. Indeed, it will help you to map out the way forward for your next 100 days, and to find out what support you need to continue to raise your game.

Building in Resilience – Exercise

This is a really simple exercise to complete but one of the most thought provoking, as it will make you think long and hard about your daily practice. Download the worksheet from *ZeroToAuthenticHero.com*, and complete each section to include what you are going to do each day to build in sustainability.

Part 1: Start with *Soul,* and work through *Physical*, *Mental*, and *Social*, listing a few things you are committing to do each day. Make sure that your activities are specific, measureable, achievable, realistic, and time-bound. If this is new to you, or you just want to improve your current practice, take a small step at first, and then build up over a period of weeks or months.

Make sure that there is balance between each area: meditating daily will undoubtedly bring great benefits, but nourishing your body and meeting friends will also bring their own benefits.

a. Soul

b. Physical

c. Mental

d. Social

Part 2: Create an accountability process. This is a way for you to ask for help from another person and check in with them on a regular basis. Using clear communication, ask for their support and a structured approach, without excuse or blame; this is an incredibly powerful process to help keep you on track. Check in with a partner, friend, or your coach.

BUILDING IN RESILIENCE

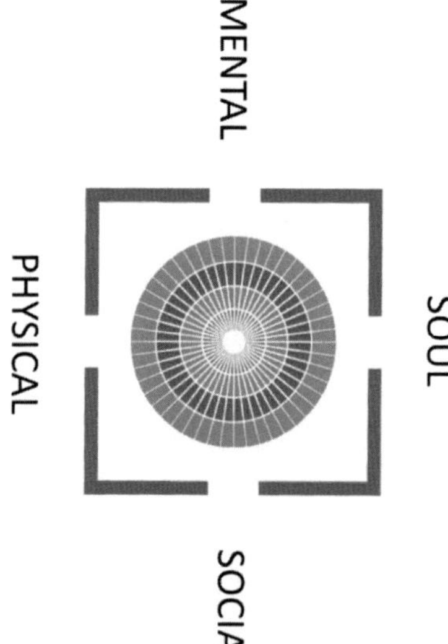

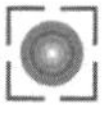

BUILDING IN RESILIENCE - PLAN

	Soul	Physical	Mental	Social
1	Meditate for 10 minutes using the headspace app every morning after brushing my teeth	Run three times a week building up to being able to run a half marathon by September	Volunteer at a women's charity to feel like I'm giving something back and gaining new skills in the process	Meet with my best friend for a good natter at least once a fortnight
2	Stop, put down my phone and engage with my children for 1 hour a day	Practice yoga for at least 10 minutes five times a week	Read one non fiction book a month	Stop for coffee with a colleague at least once a week
3	Keep all notifications turned off on my phone so they do not distract me from being focused and present.	Ensure I stop and eat a healthy lunch every day whilst not staring at a screen	Continue to read the monthly Harvard Business Review beyond the end of my studies	Attend a College event once a month
4		Eat breakfast every day	Read Times Higher Education weekly	Join a running club, rather than just stalking their pages on Facebook

Accountability Process: Share process with friends and ask them to join me

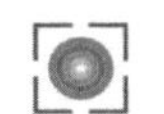

Notes

Notes

The 100-Day Plan

"This is the true joy in life, the being used for a purpose recognised by yourself as a mighty one; the being a force of nature instead of a feverish, selfish little clod of ailments and grievances, complaining that the world will not devote itself to making you happy. I am of the opinion that my life belongs to the whole community, and as long as I live, it is my privilege to do for it whatever I can."
George Bernard Shaw, Irish playwright.

Whether you have taken each of the 7 steps individually—or you have jumped in with both feet and tackled everything at once—you will have a number of worksheets and action plans, and this is the place to bring them all together.

There have been 7 steps, and there has been much change, so this may well feel a little overwhelming. It is usual to work through these every 10–14 days, over an initial 100-day period, but even now, there is the opportunity to bring all of those 7 steps together, and develop a further 100-day plan to really ingrain the learning, practice the actions, and grow in awareness and authenticity.

This is also the place to make one clear plan going forward for the next 100 days, and to find out how to receive ongoing support from the Mandala Leaders Circle, which is a community of other leaders who have been through this process and have made a commitment to support others.

How Do You Eat an Elephant?

All of this change may feel intimidating or exciting, scary or challenging, but there is much to do. When there is a challenge that seems too big to get your arms around, I usually ask a simple question: how do you eat an elephant?

This metaphor should make you think about how to swallow something that will obviously fill our stomachs easily; and, actually, there are two answers.

The first answer—the answer I would usually give when faced with this challenge—is to eat it one leg at a time. Here, you break down the elephant into smaller parts—body, head, each of the legs, etc.—and tackle them one at a time.

The second answer—and this is the first time that this answer has ever been revealed—is to invite the whole village to join the feast. In this way, you ask others for help and build a team of supporters around you who will have your back when you tackle the seemingly overwhelming problem. This could be friends, family, your boss, a mentor, or—much better— a coach!!

Live the Authentic You—Every Day

Live it every day. At first, there may only be small incremental changes, although there will be some great examples of where the changes have a beneficial impact. However, only you can make change for yourself—and you can't make others change. You have to work hard at it and invest the time, money, and effort to make it work.

At this stage, it's worth checking in to see how much willpower you have in order to achieve these changes, this personal growth. Score yourself on the strength of your will, between 1 and 10.

What's your score? 1 2 3 4 5 6 7 8 9 10

Did you score 1–4? If your willpower is in this range, then there are serious issues at play. However, let me invite you to think about it this way: what was your willpower at the start of this program? It must have been at least in the middle of the range, as you have managed to complete the 7 steps. Congratulations; you have greater willpower than you allow yourself to believe. Maybe it's worth revisiting some of the steps and coming back to this stage, or maybe it's worth getting a coach.

Did you score 5–6? If you did, then you are doing well, but there is room for improvement. Ask yourself why you didn't score a 3 or 4. Is it because you actually have many of the skills and resources that you need? Do you actually have the ability to do this but are still holding yourself back? Do you need coaching support? Give yourself credit for your abilities, and reaffirm your skills; then, ask yourself again what your score is.

Did you score 7–8? That's great; but why not 9 or 10? Is it a question of more time, more money, or more knowledge to get there? What are you missing? What else do you need? Do you need clarity? Consider this: it's not the resources that you have but how resourceful you are with them. Think how to tackle the issue with a different approach. Now, how's your score?

Did you score 9–10? This is great. Well played. Get cracking. However, please do also pay special attention to step 7 and how to build resilience, as whenever we play in our upper range for prolonged periods of time, we can tire out more easily, get frustrated by others' lack of commitment or, in many cases, of alpha's just simply getting bored and moving on.

So, score yourself every day, and keep track of how you are doing; and, most important, why you have scored high or low.

What activities, beliefs, or feelings are moving your scores, and which do you want to do less, and which more?

Reflection

You will, by now, have all of the tools you need to become a Truly Authentic Leader.

However, the next 100 days are crucial to continue to grow in authenticity by practicing what you have learnt, and to take the actions you have committed to yourself and others through the 7 steps. The exercise on the following pages will help you to build a plan, maintain focus, and check your progress each day. Ask for help, and maintain an accountability process too.

Mandala Leaders Circle

I invite everyone who reads this book, or works through an online program, joins one of my events, or works with me personally, to join the Mandala Leaders Circle. When you have joined the circle, you will have access to hundreds of other authentic leaders who have been involved with the 7 steps and have made a commitment to support you leaders on your journey.

The only conditions of entry are:

1. You have completed one of the programs.
2. You make a firm public commitment to support others.

It's called a circle as there is no hierarchy: each leader is equal regardless of their experience, the size of the organization they work for, their title, or where in the world they work. The reason we do this is to live one of the core values: equal dignity. This is a safe place for you to share your learning, challenges, and obstacles, or to simply ask for help.

In addition, you will receive regular wisdom on leadership, and early access to new programs and events. This is also a great place to network with and meet other leaders in your field, or elsewhere, and connect with them. To access the Mandala Leaders Circle, go to ZeroToAuthenticHero.com, and follow *Bonuses.*

PS. How do you eat an elephant—there is no intention to offend elephant lovers or, indeed, vegetarians—it's only a metaphor.

PPS. No elephants were eaten in the writing of this book.

100-Day Plan - Exercise

Think about the key learnings you have taken for the 7 steps, and what the key actions are that you have been practicing and wish to grow and improve. Download the worksheet from ZeroToAuthenticHero.com, which you can complete online or print and fill in by hand. However, this is a very large worksheet, so I recommend printing on A3 paper, or larger, and using it as a poster on your wall.

The worksheet shows the 7 steps across the top; select up to 3 actions you want to progress in each step, and record them here. Then, working up from the bottom, state what you are going to do each day to continue your personal development.

I would recommend that you have a maximum of 5 or 6 actions each day, so spread them out across the steps each day, and build a routine—for example, going to the gym every Wednesday—checking in with my strategy every Friday, etc., etc.

It may be that you have to practice what will be the same each day—for example, using nonviolent communication, or meditating—so you could just block out that box, as it doesn't need specific direction; you just do the same each day.

That being said, don't try and eat all the elephant at once. Maybe just practice every couple of days to start, and build up over a period of time. If you have a regular daily practice, change it occasionally—go to a yoga group as opposed to doing it alone at home—talk to somebody else to receive feedback as opposed to just scoring yourself.

There are also review days scheduled every 10th day; take the opportunity to review the next 10 days, and see what you need to adjust or increase to accelerate growth.

Check in every day with that day's plan, and try to do them early in the day—you will soon see the benefits for the remainder of that day when you have made great progress on yourself first—remember the story about putting on your oxygen mask first so that you can better help others.

Score yourself every day, and keep track of how you are doing; and, most important, why you have scored high or low. What activities, beliefs, or feelings are moving your scores, and which do you want to do less, and which more? I suggest you review every 10 days how you are doing, and change the plan for the next week to be in line with your overall goals.

Create an accountability process. This is a way for you to ask for help from another person and check in with them on a regular basis. Using clear communication, ask for their support and a structured approach, without excuse or blame; this is an incredibly powerful process to help keep you on track.

Most important, however, is the wisdom that this is not a journey you take alone. Include your partner, family, friends, and colleagues, in parts of the plan. Join a networking group, jump into the Mandala Leaders Circle, or get a coach.

THE 100 DAY PLAN

THE 100 DAY PLAN

Notes

References & Links

Step 1: Understanding Your Beliefs

I was first told the story of the eagle and the chicken when it was told by Preethaji, at the One World Academy, a Wisdom School for Enlightenment. It is based on a new tradition, where the focus is on knowing oneself and discovering that we are connected to all that exists.
http://www.oneworldacademy.com/

Step 2: Having a Clear Purpose

I was delighted to find the approaches of Southwest Airlines, and Starbucks, as inspiration here, but I chose to build my own process to gain real clarity on the purpose.
Southwest Airlines:
https://www.youtube.com/watch?v=eGxMf88I5g4
Starbucks: https://www.youtube.com/watch?v=EdmTG1OZ2ew

Step 3: Living Your Core Values

The original thoughts about the four core values I practice came from Jasper Juul, who runs the Family Lab International (FLI), where they teach professionals and parents to work together to figure out how to transform emotional love and commitment into loving behaviour.
http://www.family-lab.com/

Step 4: Improving Your Skill Set

I first heard the story of the elephant and the tree when it was told by Preethaji, at the One World Academy, a Wisdom School for Enlightenment. It is based on a new tradition, where the focus is on knowing oneself and discovering that we are connected to all that exists.
http://www.oneworldacademy.com/

The exercise here was first demonstrated by Gregor Schill, of Schill Coaching. He coaches individuals and groups, and holds lectures on coaching, coaching leadership, and mental training, as well as education in these subjects. Gregor also works a lot with peak performance in sports.
https://schillcoaching.se/

Step 5: Communicating With Clarity

The story asking who smashed the well was taught to me by Mike Crofts, who was formerly a Captain in the Royal Army Tank Regiment of the British Army, and is now CEO of the 3 Pillars Project, which takes rugby to prisons, in order to teach values through exercise, education, and ethos.
https://www.3pillarsproject.com/

The use of *I language* was first demonstrated to me by the Mankind Project, which is a global brotherhood of non-profit, charitable organisations that conduct challenging and highly rewarding programs for men at every stage of life.
https://mankindproject.org/

<u>Step 6: Living Your Legacy</u>

I was introduced to the legacy process by Daniel Frohwein, which was the classic process of imagining yourself on your deathbed and planning what you wanted to achieve before actually reaching this time. I chose to adapt it, influenced by John Glenn's quote:

"I'm not interested in my legacy. I made up a word: live-acy. I'm more interested in living."

<u>Step 7: Building in Resilience</u>

The story of the phoenix rising from the ashes was referred to in an article by Parul Sehgal, a literary critic whose articles have been published in numerous literary magazines and newspapers, including the *New York Times Book Review* and the *New York Times*.

https://www.nytimes.com/2015/12/06/magazine/the-profound-emptiness-of-resilience.html

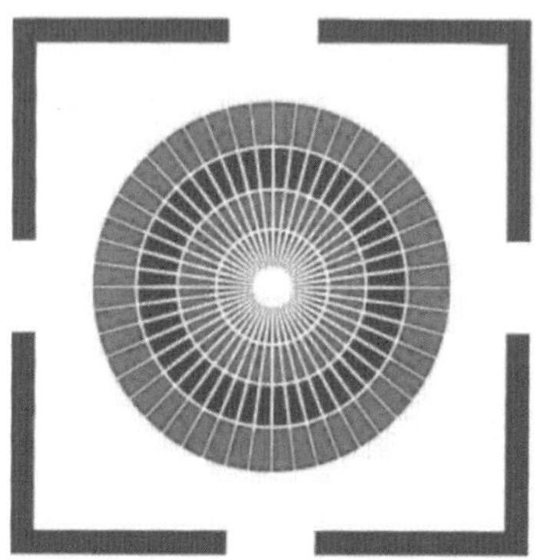

ZERO TO AUTHENTIC HERO

THE 7 KEY STEPS TO BECOME A TRUE LEADER